LABOUR AND CHANGE

LABOUR AND CHANGE

Essays on Globalization, Technological
Change and Labour in India

Kuriakose Mamkoottam

Los Angeles I London I New Delhi
Singapore I Washington DC I Melbourne

First published in 2003 by

SAGE Publications India Pvt Ltd
B1/I-1 Mohan Cooperative Industrial Area
Mathura Road, New Delhi 110 044, India
www.sagepub.in

SAGE Publications Inc
2455 Teller Road
Thousand Oaks, California 91320, USA

SAGE Publications Ltd
1 Oliver's Yard, 55 City Road
London EC1Y 1SP, United Kingdom

SAGE Publications Asia-Pacific Pte Ltd
3 Church Street
#10-04 Samsung Hub
Singapore 049483

Published by Vivek Mehra for SAGE Publications India Pvt Ltd, typeset in CalistoMT 10.5/12 by S.R. Enterprises, New Delhi.

Library of Congress Cataloging-in-Publication Data

Mamkoottam, Kuriakose
    Labour and change: essays on globalization, technological change and labour in India/Kuriakose Mamkoottam.
        p. cm.
    Includes bibliographical references (p.   ) and index.
    1. Organizational change—India.   2. Employees—Effect of technological innovations on—India   3. Industrial relations—India. 4. Globalization.   I. Title.

HD 58.8.M2454 2003   658.4´06—dc21   2002156175

ISBN: 978-07-619-9742-9 (PB)

SAGE Team: Medha Dube, Roshni Basu, R.A.M. Brown and Santosh Rawat

Contents

Preface

This volume on labour and change is a collection of revised papers, originally written by the author over the past five years. The main theme of the book is change, and how the process of change is closely linked to people and organizations. Unless organizations are equipped with adequate knowledge, besides the appropriate skills and attitudes, they will not be able to adapt to the challenges of the changing environment. Organizations can build the capability to cope with change only if their members are willing to accept and intiate change.

The last quarter of the 20th century will be remembered for the massive changes that have transformed the world and our worldviews. Technological change, in particular, has influenced every walk of life, including every aspect of industry, be it manufacturing or services, private or public, domestic or multinational. The much acclaimed process of globalization has left few countries and companies untouched.

During this period, most economies undertook policy changes, some radical in nature, to usher in economic liberalization and internationalization of products and services. Global markets and international competition became realities. In the face of severe competititon from the global market, India too, adopted a path of structural change in the early 1990s. The process was initiated by the announcement of the 'new economic policy' in 1991. This volume addresses the various aspects of technological, economic and organizational changes that have taken place in the liberalized India of the post-1990 period, as well as their implications for labour and organizations.

Chapter 1 discusses the criticality of change and the role that human resource management can play in managing it. The importance of the management (leadership, in particular), and the upgradation of technology and knowledge are the focus of this introductory chapter.

Chapter 2 deals with the process of globalization, and the close link between technology, human resources (labour) and globalization. Their effect on each other has also been discussed, with particular reference to the symbiotic relationship between technology and labour. The chapter examines various facets of microelectronics, as well as its impact on organizational and occupational structures, knowledge, skills and employment in the contemporary Indian context.

The structural changes undertaken in India in the early 1990's together with their impact on labour and trade unions, are the subject of Chapter 3. After dealing with the nature of industrial relations and trade unionism, the chapter goes on to discuss their impact on technological change and globalization on the one hand, and the latter's influence on the former, on the other. Organizational culture plays an important role in bringing about change. In this context, the evolution of a system of shared goals, values and beliefs is of crucial significance.

Chapter 4 examines two case studies which illustrate that change initiatives will not succeed unless they are accompanied by an appropriate cultural transformation among the employees of an organization.

Concerns regarding productivity are not new. However, globalization and the increasingly competitive environment have spurred economies and organizations to focus on improving productivity with renewed vigour. Productivity bargaining made its appearance as early as 1960 with the Fawley agreement in Great Britain. Chapter 5 examines a number of productivity agreements, taken from a sample of companies representing the public as well as private sector, including multinationals. An analysis of these agreements shows that companies use the process of productivity bargaining to initiate changes, including technological innovation and organizational reform.

Chapter 6 deals with the intimate relationship between change and industrial relations. It dwells on the experiences of different countries, such as Japan, Germany and the Scandinavian countries, in the sphere of industrial relations. This discussion of the various systems evolved illustrates that it is easier to introduce change if industrial relations are marked by a spirit of co-operation, especially in a competitive environment.

All efforts to change are based on a recognition of the need to improve. It is also important to recognize that no change is possible without the involvement and commitment of the employees. The final chapter attempts to explain the importance of this factor, using the theoretical concepts of *power, involvement* and *commitment.*

Kuriakose Mamkoottam

1
Managing Change: Issues and Concerns

Introduction

Change is an all-pervasive and permanent reality. It knows no boundaries of time and space. Through the centuries, scholars and thinkers have enquired into the causes and consequences of change, which may be political, social, technological or scientific in nature. However, it may not be an exaggeration to suggest that the changes witnessed in recent decades have been of such a radical nature that they have created a break in the history of modern man. As Peters (2000) says, the world is changing more fundamentally than it has in hundreds of years. Peters predicts that 90 per cent of white-collar jobs in the US will be either destroyed or altered beyond recognition in the next 10 to 15 years. This is a catastrophic prediction, given the fact that 90 per cent of the country's working population is engaged in white-collar work of one sort or another. Even most manufacturing jobs these days are connected to such white-collar services as finance, human resources and engineering.

Change is a given factor in the contemporary organizational context, and its management is critical to the success and survival of an organization. It is important to gain an understanding of the principles and nature of change, both at the individual and group levels, if we are to appreciate its implication and become a part of the change process. Burke et al. (1993) examined the awareness among managers and executives of the process of change management. They administered the Managing Change Questionnaire (developed by W. Warner Burke Associates, Inc.), to 700 managers and executives from a cross-section of organizations in order to make a quantitative assessment of their knowledge. The results indicated that these individuals would have received a grade of "C" in the subject of managing change. This does not bode well, considering the fact that it is these very men who are instrumental in shaping the future of their organizations. The authors found that the managers had two weak spots, in particular. First, there was a gap in their knowledge of individual responses to the efforts made at change. Second, they were not well-versed in those areas of change that relate to the management of people. In other words, the managers had difficulty interpreting their employees' reactions and were, therefore, likely to face problems in guiding them through the often complex and confusing process of change.

Change in an organization involves altering its structure, processes, the behaviour of its management and staff, its strategy, the environment, and so on. The organization's structure is perhaps one of the most common targets of change. This would cover the manner in which it is held together, the various configurations of people and the relationships between them, communication channels, job roles and skills. The relationships within an organization are extremely important because they give it internal shape and coherence. As for processes, they may be seen as sequences of related activities within an organization, which transform inputs into outputs. Manufacturing processes and the interaction with customers involve detailed sequencing of activities and events. Some other processes which are the targets of change are as follows:

- Communication processes—formal or informal—for disseminating information and knowledge within the organization.
- Management processes which govern the manner in which decisions are made, as well as the allocation of work and resources.
- Learning processes, which should help an organization learn from its past, and through its customers, competitors and staff. Recently, concepts like 'knowledge management', 'soft systems dynamics' and 'action learning' have been used to deepen our understanding of (organizational) learning.

Behaviour, another important area of change, may be defined in terms of the patterns of action and reaction within the organization. These are influenced by the organization's culture, a term which describes the collective preference or shared mind-set that determines 'the way things get done'. The other targets of change in the sphere of behaviour include the manner in which employees deal with uncertainty, the changing expectations or values of customers, and of society as a whole.

Crucial to any organization are its corporate objectives, strategies and the basis on which it is to compete in a given market. Periodic reviews of the goals are vital if an organization is to stay aligned with the demands of the market and the shareholders' expectations. Most organizations are constantly trying to make some change or other in their internal environment in order to ensure success in the future. The changes are planned largely by the management, which must adopt a proactive policy to keep the organization going.

If all the above-mentioned changes were carried out, it would affect the overall state of the organization. An organization's state may be measured in terms of the cash flow, annual turnover, share price, return on the capital employed, or market share. Kaplan and Norton (1992) suggest that an organization should attempt to set up a measurement to monitor organizational performance in four key areas. These are:

- Business processes
- Innovation and learning
- Finance
- Customer satisfaction

A drop in performance or a raised level of performance by the competitors in any of these areas may necessitate the introduction of changes. In fact, to succeed in today's competitive environment, it is necessary for organizations to anticipate the future and initiate changes proactively.

Whenever possible, change occurs along the lines of least resistance. Most often, it takes paths where there is little to impede it. Amorphous systems, which do not have a proper formal structure or internal framework, are the ones that can change more easily. Change is most likely to take place in situations where there is little resistance to it. An organization's structure and operational rigidity are important factors in this context. The structural boundaries and clear lines of symmetry define the areas in which change is most likely to occur with ease. Resistance to change may be visible within organizations whose business is self-contained, such as family-controlled or public sector organizations. Such organizations are largely inward-looking and parochial. Their major concern is maintaining the purity and sanctity of company procedures and processes, rather than adjusting to the needs of a changing market/environment. This may partly explain why companies in India, which consist largely of family-owned private enterprises and state-owned public sector enterprises, have been slow to change.

However, developments in recent years have reinforced the view of Stickland (1998), who believes that we are moving from a world in which we determined our destination to one in which we must learn to navigate a path between myriad future possibilities. In this world, we should never set our strategic sights too far ahead. There are now few givens and absolutes around which we can base our path of change. What is urgently required is a sound understanding of the workings of change, and of what drives it and shapes it within our organizations. Fundamentally, change is the engine, which propels an organization from the cloying affections of the past, through the challenges of the present and into the future.

Talking about the challenges of change and the need for new competencies and mind-sets, Morgan (1989) had, a decade ago, outlined different possible scenarios that could arise in the future with respect to the intensity of change. He visualized an increasingly turbulent environment. Indeed, few organizations can be sure of a secure future, as scientific and technological developments are transforming the very ground on which they have learned to operate. As Morgan foresaw, the world is in a greater flux today than ever before. Organizations and their managers must recognize the need to develop new mindsets, skills and abilities which will help them cope with this flux. Morgan suggested that the increasing turbulence would necessitate the adoption of a more proactive and entrepreneurial policy within the organization. Organizations would have to learn to anticipate and manage emergent problems. They would also need to formulate new initiatives and give a new direction to their development. The proactive approach advocated by Morgan is essential for empowering and energizing an organization to cope with the challenges facing it.

Change and Managing Human Resources

Organizational change has to be seen in association with the character and style of management, in general, and the organization's leadership, in particular. In recent years, the role of the leadership has assumed greater importance at all levels of an organization. Leadership has also undergone a change in character, from being (highly) formalized or hierarchical to being dynamic and people-centred (decentralized). Increasingly, the leadership process is becoming identified with an ability to mobilize the energies and gain the commitment of the staff, through the creation of shared values and mutual understandings. Today's manager has to view leadership as a 'framing' and 'bridging' process—a process which should energize the employees and focus their efforts in ways that resonate with the demands posed by the wider environment. In the modern age, knowledge, creativity, opportunity-seeking, interpersonal skills, and entrepreneurial ability are becoming important. The corporate world is becoming increasingly driven by knowledge and information. The management of human resources becomes extremely important in a society in which knowledge and information enjoy a premium. Thus, a manager has to find ways of tapping the intelligence, knowledge and creative potential of each employee at every level of the organization. This, in turn, requires the development of organizational processes and structures which promote these qualities. Learning and innovation are an obvious part of the process.

Organizations must also develop more open managerial processes, which flatten hierarchies and improve lateral interactions.

The ability to manage and work within multidisciplinary teams is essential. The flattening of the organizational structure must be synchronized with new approaches to management and control. As the rigidity and hierarchy of bureaucratic structures become less relevant, managers will have to learn to coordinate through the development of a system of shared values. They will need to find the right balance between delegation and control. This necessarily means decentralization, and for this purpose, a manager must become capable of designing and managing systems which are self-organizing. The management should be more concerned with empowerment than with close supervision and control.

The pace of change and the development of skills necessitated by this make the process of continuous learning essential. Information technology (IT), in the form of micro-computing, robotics, electronic communication and the internet, has transformed the nature and structure of many organizations. It has also brought about major alterations in the nature and life-cycles of the various products and services. This age of technology is leading to the emergence of completely new styles of organization and human resource competencies. Organizational hierarchies must now give way to organizational units which are loosely coupled and of a smaller scale. They need to be coordinated electronically, so that the work units can remain separate, yet integrated.

Though many managers may want simplicity, the reality is that they have to deal with increasingly complex situations. The complexity of organizational life is increasing rather than decreasing, as manifested in the conflicting demands posed by multiple stakeholders. Today, the different shareholders—employees, unions, customers, collaborating firms, government agencies, the local community and the general public—interact with each other as active stakeholders in the organization, each imposing its own demands on the management. Thus, managers have to continuously hone their skills in managing transition, recognizing flux as the norm. This entails the development of mind-sets and skills which allow them to cope with the continuous flow of new ideas, products, technologies, skills and information, besides the dynamics of interpersonal and inter-organizational relations. Managers at the top/senior level will have to take much greater social responsibility, not just for lofty moral reasons, but because it is a necesssity in a complex, interdependent society. A manager will now have to think about his organization and its relationships in a wider context.

Change and Technology

Globalization and the widespread application of microelectronics, besides that of the internet, are associated with the radical changes which have taken place recently. The widespread use of IT has accelerated the generation and transmission of information, making communication more efficient than ever before. It is also argued that the easy availability of information and faster communication have, in their turn, accelerated the process of globalization. Information technology is revolutionizing the way we communicate, work, shop and play. Computers and the internet are paving the way for a sweeping reorganization of business, from online procurement of inputs to greater decentralization and out-sourcing. By increasing access to information, IT has made the working of markets more efficient. The impact of IT is truly global. More and more knowledge can be stored and sent to any destination in the world, at a negligible cost. Information technology and globalization are intimately interconnected. By reducing the cost of communications, IT has helped globalize production and the capital markets. Globalization, in turn, further accelerates competition and innovation. It also speeds up the diffusion of new technology through trade and investment.

International competition among nation states and corporate firms to dominate the global market have created a struggle for survival, in which constant innovation and continuous improvement play a major role. Firms have always been forced to change due to factors in their environment, as well as technological factors. As McLoughlin and Harris (1997) suggest, firms are driven to innovate primarily by technological imperatives and the demands of competition. They have little choice in the matter if they wish to survive. In particular, international competition has conditioned the way sociologists and others seek to understand the impact of computer-based technological change on variables such as skills, job content, work organization, employees, attitudes and behaviour, and organizational structure and design. However, the developments taking place today cannot be seen as giving rise to a unidirectional process. The attitudes of the management and workers, organizational structures, cultural systems, industrial relations, and the wider social and political environment may act as either facilitators or hindrances to technological change and globalization.

Technology is not value-neutral. In this context, McLoughlin and Harris (1997) have identified several problem areas. First, technological innovations are often seen to arise in a more or less neutral way, out of the activities of inventors, professional research or development laboratories. However, critics view it differently. They argue that the form and direction of technological innovation should be seen as a product of the direct influence of social and political factors, not least the interests of the state and employers. Second, those who believe in a technological imperative assume that managers play the role of unreflective 'messengers', whose task is to read the technological and commercial signals emanating from the firm's environment and take appropriate action. Critics, on the other hand, argue that managers should be seen as 'creative mediators', whose choices critically influence the ways in which particular technological and market options are selected for development. Third, it is assumed that in the long run, technological innovation inevitably benefits everybody. The employers, management, workers and unions are believed to have a common interest in ensuring technological progress. However, technological innovation is often an area in which interests diverge. If new technologies are designed and used to serve particular interests, and if an organization is seen not as an arena of consensus but as a locus of conflict, then disagreements over particular technical changes are an inevitable, legitimate feature of organizational life. As we shall discuss in the subsequent chapters, technological changes and their implications become the centre of conflict in many Indian organizations.

There are broadly two views on a human being's ability to influence the magnitude and direction of change within a system. According to the first, the environment dictates human activities, in the short as well as long term. The phenomenon of change in human behaviour is, therefore, viewed as mechanistic and deterministic in nature. It is caused and shaped by external forces beyond the control of the individuals within the system. According to Stickland (1998), change can take place regardless of our perception of it, and it can go beyond human control or comprehension. This, in other words, means that human or social choice does not have much of a role in determining change. In fact, Heraclitus, a philosopher in 500 BC, held the extreme position that 'you cannot step into the same river twice, for fresh waters are always flowing in upon you'. Thus, according to this view, change is a constant reality, and is also something over which man has no control at all.

According to the second view, human systems are largely autonomous and individuals possess a free will. Changes in behaviour stem from individual impetus and are spontaneous in origin. There is immense potential for a wide variety of change, which may be highly unpredictable. In fact, one may extend this view to suggest that the emerging behaviour patterns and changes at the organization level of the whole, possibly affect the external environment over time.

The reality, however, may lie somewhere between these two extreme views. While some changes may be imposed from outside, others may be initiated from within the organization. However, it must be said that, it would be difficult to identify changes that cannot be associated with some external force or the other. It is, therefore, widely accepted that the structure and culture of an organization must respond to the demands of the environment if it is to survive in the long term.

Knowledge and Change

Modern-day economies are increasingly based on knowledge. A growing portion of today's economy is in the form of intangibles, based on the use of ideas rather than material things. Only one-third of American workers were employed in the service sector in 1900, compared to more than three-quarters in 2000. Thinking is serious business today. Academicians and practitioners alike acknowledge the importance of understanding the thinking processes within an organization. It is now well recognized that only knowledge and its management determine success or failure, and, therefore, cognition is an important process.

There are two approaches to organizational thinking—behavioural and cognitive. According to the behavioural approach, it is not possible to study and understand the mental state of the people; we can understand only their behaviour and responses to different stimuli. Change is reactive; it is a matter of external and environmental influences. The cognitive approach looks at the internal complexity of the learners and analyses their behaviour in the context of their mental states. Learning is a proactive process of acting and gradually building on one's environment. It precedes change. Every learning event inevitably has a framework. An organization designs its activities to suit its corporate goals and strategies, while individual participants have their own subjective goals and strategies to achieve these.

All successful attempts at managing organizational change have two basic elements in common. One, there is a strong change agent or change manager to initiate the process of change. Two, the change process covers four key areas—its culture, operations, structure and strategy, including its strategy for the management of human resources. However, the biggest factor in managing change is the management of the people involved in the process. One of the factors which is largely missing in today's global organization is trust. Winning the trust of the people during the implementation of changes is of vistal importance. In several organizations, it has been observed that most employees want to know what is going to happen next. Very often, employees suddenly stop trusting the organization in the middle of the change process, as the ground rules begin to change one by one. As we shall see in later chapters, the employees do not trust the intentions of the management, and this suspicion often develops into interdepartmental and interfunctional conflict. Thus, predictability is an important factor in the eyes of the employees.

The impact of change must be communicated to the employees as the organization seeks to move towards new organizational goals. Organizations that carry out strategic, organizational and other changes often tie up their programmes to the core competencies of their personnel. Managers must define the capabilities of the employees much in the same way that an organization needs to define its core competence. If an employee has a clear idea of what is required of him, he will be better equipped to handle the responsibilities assigned to him in the process of change. Very often, a diverse array of skills is required for an organization to make the transition, and no one employee possesses all these skills simultaneously. Thus, it is important to develop interdependency.

Modern organizations built on the model of Weberian bureaucracy are accustomed to placing trust in the system rather than on the people in it. In fact, people are expected to fit into the system to ensure success. However, with the passage of time, unexpected events have overtaken most organizations and their systems have been hard put to coping with the changing realities. Gradually, organizations have realized the need to rely increasingly on their employees to make decisions on matters for which a systematic (routine) response may not suffice. As Kanter (1983) says, after years of telling corporate citizens to 'trust the system', many companies must now learn to trust their staff. They have to encourage their employees to use their latent creative capacities, which have been neglected so far, in order to tap the most potent economic stimulus of all: idea power. In other words, it is the individual who is capable of moving the organization into the more uncertain realm of innovation, thus taking the organization beyond what it already knows and helping it keep in step with the environment. An organization can alter its internal environment to empower and stimulate its employees to act. It can systematically encourage innovation by the way it designs its system and treats its staff. The degree to which individuals are granted or deprived of the opportunity to use power effectively is one operative difference between those companies which innovate and those which stagnate.

The term 'innovation' is not confined to (new) technology, (new) products or (new) methods of making them. Innovation is the process of bringing into use any new idea for solving a problem. Ideas for reorganizing, cutting costs, improving communication, or building effective teams are all innovations. Innovation is the generation, acceptance and implementation of new ideas, processes, products or services. Today's changing world requires as much social and organizational innovation as technical innovation. In fact, if technical innovation runs far ahead of social and organizational innovation, which are complementary to it, its use in practice can turn out to be either negligible, or it may prove to be dysfunctional. We shall see in a later chapter that technical change does not yield the desired results unless it is introduced in tandem with changes in an organization's structure, and the competencies and attitudes of its staff.

Stickland (1998) identifies three fundamental sources/categories of change: information, action and process. Access to information can be a cause of change. Rapid communication and transmission of information can cause a series of cascading changes within large composite systems. Action consists of specific acts which can be attribued to a particular part of the organization and located at a given, fixed moment in time. The ensuing change could affect the organization in which the action originated, or other organizations. Decision making falls under this category, as it can be seen both as a cognitive act in itself, as well as an act which results in specific behavioural actions. Process can be defined as a connected series of actions attributable to one or more parts of an organizational system, or the whole, occurring over time. Over time, there may be a causal link from information to action, and on to process. Nonetheless, each category in itself can represent a specific, individual source of change. Together, these three categories are proposed as a simple analytical base upon which one can describe the sources of both internal and external change within an organization.

Approaches to Change

The most important aspect of managing change is the choice of an appropriate strategy and its implementation. An organization is more likely to succeed in this if it has clearly identified the stakeholders involved in the change process and assessed the impact of the proposed changes on them. According to Carnall (1995), the stakeholders must be made aware of any change in strategy. It must also be ensured that they accept the implications of the change and that they are capable of coping with it. It is important to see to it that the stakeholders understand and believe in the vision, the strategy and the plan for implementing the change. The stakeholders involved should believe that they are capable of developing the necessary skills to cope with the change and take full advantage of it. They must be capable of developing new attitudes and ways of working. It is necessary that they value the new jobs and opportunities coming their way.

Beer and Nohria (2000) note that never since the Industrial Revolution have the stakes of dealing with change been so high. Most traditional organizations have accepted, at least in theory, that they must either change or die. The process of ushering in change remains one of the most difficult things to accomplish— few organizations manage it as well as they would like to. Most initiatives in introducing new technology, restructuring, downsizing or transforming corporate culture have had a poor success rate. Many change initiatives meet with failures that prove fatal. On the basis of very different, and often unconscious, assumptions about why and how changes should be made, Beer and Nohria propose two archetypes of change, namely, theory E and theory O. Theory E pertains to change based on economic value, and theory O to change based on the organization's capability. Theory E is known as the hard approach, and is the more commonly adopted one. It is intended to enhance the shareholder value. It is a top-down approach and the leaders who subscribe to it manage change in the old-fashioned way. They believe that goals can be accomplished without really involving their management teams, and certainly without any inputs from the lower levels or unions.

By contrast, participation is the hallmark of theory O, which is known as the soft approach. The initial focus of this theory is on building up the organization's 'software', i.e. the culture, behaviour and attitudes of the employees. The thrust is on developing corporate culture and human capability through the process of learning, both at the individual and organizational levels. Thus, theory O attempts to achieve a cultural transformation. The process of change is facilitated by obtaining feedback, reflecting and making further changes. Companies which adopt O strategies typically have the strong and long-standing commitment of their employees. Such commitment is based on psychological contracts made with the employees in the past. Hewlett–Packard provides an example of this type of strategy, which it adopted when its performance began flagging in the 1980s. The managers of such companies are likely to see the risks of breaking those implicit contracts. Asian and European businesses are also more likely to adopt an O strategy for change because they see the value of having the employees' commitment. However, according to Beer and Nohria (2000), most companies use a mix of the two theories. Companies which effectively combine the hard and soft approaches can reap large benefits in terms of profitability and productivity. These companies are likely to gain a sustainable competitive advantage.

The winds of change began sweeping the developed economies and many of the newly developing/developed economies, including China and the south-east Asian countries, in the late 1970s and early 1980s. However, India's economy and its corporate sector began to realize the impact of the new wave, as well as the urgency of the need to change only by the late 1980s and early 1990s. By then, the gap between the developed world and India—in terms of technology, productivity, income levels, the availability of new products and services and their quality—had widened. A myriad of factors may have contributed to this ever-growing gap. However, one can perhaps isolate certain factors as major ones. The following chapters seek to demonstrate that labour, industrial relations and the management of people may be among the crucial issues that affect an organization's success in coping with challenges. Each of the following chapters deals with different areas of change, such as globalization, re-structuring, an organization's culture, productivity bargaining and employees' commitment. However, the major concern of this book is to explore the symbiotic relationship between people (labour), organizations and change.

As Carnall (1995) says, 'To achieve change, we must first recognize that change is desirable and feasible. We must get people to recognize that changes are needed.' People will get a better idea of the picture if they appreciate the fact that the various dimensions of change, particularly technological change, are intimately interlinked with labour and human resource management in organizations. The following chapters attempt to throw some light on this aspect.

Sumantra Ghoshal et al. (2000) have observed in their recent book, 'After almost a decade since India took the first tentative steps to economic liberalization in 1991, most Indian managers who have survived the traumas of industry overcapacity and restructuring, the onslaught of foreign competition, and the growing sophistication of customers and technologies, will quickly agree that companies all over the country, in all kinds of businesses, are in the midst of radical change.' However, an equally important observation would be that not many have succeeded in their endeavour to change over. For this reason, subsequent chapters of this book focus on how organizational (management) policies and practices in the spheres of technology, labour and trade unions, on the one hand, and the approach of labour and trade unions, on the other, affect the nature, direction and speed of change.

References

Beer, M., and **Nohria, N.** (2000). 'Cracking the code of change'. *Harvard Business Review*, May–June 2000, pp. 133–141.

Burke, W. W., Church, A.H. and **Waclawski, J.** (1993). 'What do OD practitioners know about managing change'? *Leadership and Organization Development Journal*, 14(6): pp. 3–11.

Carnall, C. (1995). *Managing Change in Organizations* (2nd edn.). London: Prentice Hall.

Ghoshal, S., Piramal, G. and **Bartlett, A.** (2000). *Managing Radical Change.* New Delhi: Viking.

Kaplan, R.S. and **Norton, D.P.** (1992). *The Balanced Scorecard.* Cambridge, Massachusetts: Harvard Business School Press.

Kanter, R.M. (1983). *The Change Masters.* London: George Allen and Unwin.

McLoughlin, I. and **Harris, M.** (1997). *Innovation, Organizational Change and Technology.* London: International Thomson Business Press.

Morgan, G. (1989). *Reading the Waves of Change.* San Francisco: Jossey–Bass Publishers.

Peters, T. (2000). 'What will we do for work'? *Time*, 155(20): pp. 38–40.

Stickland, F. (1998). *The Dynamics of Change.* London: Routledge.

2

Globalization, Technology and Human Resources

Introduction

The last quarter of the 20th century would be well remembered for the widely debated issues of globalization and the internationalization of economies across the world. Much of the debate has remained inconclusive even at the beginning of the new millennium. The world seems divided between those who support the process of globalization and those who, if not oppose it, have highlighted that its ill effects outweigh the advantages.

The term 'globalization' has gained universal currency, while the phenomenon itself has brought about a radical shift in the structure and functioning of contemporary industry and business. As Porter (1990) has aptly put it, globalization has come to define the competitive advantage of nations, i.e., their ability to compete and survive in the global market. As this market goes beyond national, political and cultural boundaries, one of the most enduring tests of an economy's comparative advantage is being seen in terms of its ability to be a global player. An economy can attain and sustain this only by integrating itself with the global market. Interestingly, and perhaps expectedly, a good part of the discussion on globalization has focused on the developing and newly developed economies.

Among the more important issues which have drawn the attention of policy-makers and scholars are the impact of globalization on the structure and performance of the national (domestic) economy and industry, on employment and the labour market, and on the structure of an organization and its management practices. This chapter examines some of the issues relating to globalization and technological change, besides their impact on labour/human resources, the organization of work, the occupational structure, the employment pattern and industrial relations. The discussion in this chapter is at a more general level, but the same issues will be taken up in greater detail in the subsequent chapters. The major purpose of this chapter is to outline the concepts relating to and the theoretical aspects of the issues mentioned above.

In recent years, many countries have introduced major reforms to integrate their economies into the world market. This has been spurred on by the need to cope with changes that are taking place at a speed faster than most are prepared or willing to accept. In the 1970s, only a few developing countries, primarily from East Asia, opened up their borders to flows of trade and investment capital. Subsequently, many Latin American and sub-Saharan countries, and three giant nations—China, the former Soviet Union and India—entered the global market. The last three account for nearly half of the world's labour force. According to an estimate made in the early 1990s (World Bank, 1995), it was expected that by the year 2000, fewer than 10 per cent of the world's workers would be cut off from the economic mainstream. This projection, however, has become debatable today.

In some cases, the availability of cheap labour proved to be an advantage. It was this factor which ultimately led to the success stories of Japan and, later, the Asian tigers in the global market. However, paradoxically, India's role in the world market shrank as a result of its increasing labour costs, in addition to the relatively slow pace of structural reforms, including industrial restructuring and labour (legislative) reforms. India ceased to enjoy the advantage of cheap labour, whether in textiles or in the engineering sector, although the absolute wages in the country is among the lowest. Despite the fact that wages in Japan or in other economically prosperous Asian countries are no longer low, these countries have continued to play a dominant role in the global market, largely because of factors other than cheap labour.

Low wages alone can no longer suffice for developing countries like India to gain a comparative advantage. This is because the actual labour costs have sharply declined in the developed nations as well. In the G-7 countries, the labour cost is estimated to account for less than 5 per cent of the sales value. New elements, like market trends in design, quality and packaging, delivery schedules, market positioning, sales promotion and distribution, contribute to the competitive advantage. Competitiveness has always been based on productivity. However, today, productivity is not interlinked mainly with the cost of labour; quality and flexibility have assumed greater importance.

Globalization and Technological Change

Information technology and the ever-improving facilities for communication and transportation play a major role in the process of globalization. Cross-border transport and trade have become easier today because of the resolution of many of the political conflicts, which had divided the economic world for decades. Political strategies for economic development and industrialization have changed across the world. Central planning has been abandoned in the former Soviet Union and Eastern Europe. The trade and import–export policies of most countries in Latin America, South Asia, and the Middle East are no longer designed to prevent trade. More and more countries have realized the need for a radical shift in the structure and functioning of their economies, industries and enterprises. Many developing countries have introduced programmes for major structural adjustment and economic liberalization in order to gain greater competitive advantage in the global market. Success in the global market can no longer be based on a nation's natural resources or cheap labour. Instead, a nation has to make deliberate choices in the matter of core technologies if it is to compete at the international level. Constant improvement and innovation in process technologies, the designs of products and management methods have become key variables. The concrete measures adopted in the Indian content and an assessment of their success/failure are discussed in detail in the subsequent chapters.

Historically, technology has always been a key factor in bringing about change in society. During the past few decades, however, a new range of technologies based on microelectronics have ushered in changes of a different dimension and intensity. The adoption of the new technologies not only transforms manufacturing processes and the service sector, but also brings about profound changes in the entire lifestyle of modern society. In the early 1980s, the increasingly competitive market put firms under a great deal of pressure. Companies were faced with the challenge of introducing greater flexibility and quality in production, better delivery systems and a greater stress on orienting their services to the customer. At the same time, there was a growing awareness of the potential of new manufacturing technologies for improving performance. As Bessant (1993) observes, the possibility of using such technology in an integrated, rather than direct form, had begun emerging. This would mean taking advantage of the advances in communications and networking technology in order to facilitate the emergence of linked manufacturing systems.

The emerging pattern of 'computer-integrated manufacturing' (CIM) systems opened the way for significant alterations at the level of strategy. Such systems result in improvements in the performance of not only particular tasks or functions, but also enhance the overall performance of the firm. The latter includes reduced response times, better quality control, faster development of products and lower inventory levels (Bessant, 1993). As the new technology became more advanced, it also became substantially more flexible, leading to the development of the Computer-Aided Design/Computer-Aided Manufacturing (CAD/CAM) systems. The key focus of the manufacturing environment in the 1980s and 1990s gradually came to lie on quality, design and flexibility. Firms came under growing pressure to innovate in order to utilize their investments in the most productive manner, while at the same time, providing increasingly high-quality services and products to the customer. According to Bessant et al. (1990), the challenges posed by the global market were the most daunting in the 1990s because firms were required to attain high levels of productivity and flexibility simultaneously. The new technological opportunities and the strategies posited by them helped the firm meet this challenge. In 1975–85, manufacturers in Europe and the US discovered that quality and cost-efficiency were not incompatible. The next period, spanning from 1985–95, confirmed that the traditional trade-off between flexibility and cost-efficiency was a thing of the past.

When faced with new challenges from the market, manufacturers turn to new technology. Information technology not only causes improvements in the aspects of communication and control across a broad range of manufacturing activities, but also facilitates integration, which is of prime importance. It brings together previously discrete items of equipment into more powerful, multifunctional systems. Integrated manufacturing systems involve high levels of computer-integration and help retain flexibility. The CIM technologies can be of immense help in improving effectiveness. For example, they can help reduce lead times and inventory levels, and raise the standards of quality. In their fascinating and much acclaimed book, *The Machine that Changed the World*, Womack et al. (1990) state that just as mass production swept away craft production, a new way of making things, called *lean production*, is now rapidly making mass production obsolete. The authors' worldwide study of the automotive industry showed that lean production welds the activities of everyone—from the top management to the line workers and suppliers—into a tightly integrated whole. This integrated unit can respond almost instantly to the demands of the customers. It is capable of doubling production and causing a twofold improvement in quality, while keeping the costs down. The adoption of lean technology, which will inevitably spread beyond the auto industry, is bound to change almost every industry. It will consequently affect the way we work and live. In the larger sense, it will determine the fate of companies and nations, depending on how they respond to its impact. Further, the increasingly widespread use of the internet in recent times is also expected to make dramatic changes in our mode of working and living.

However, studies show that the full benefits of the new technologies, such as the CIM, CAM, CAD, FMS (Flexible Manufacturing Systems) and CAPM (Computer-Aided Production Management) systems, cannot be taken for granted. These technologies are beneficial only if simultaneous changes are brought about in the organization's physical lay-out, its structure and work culture, and in the skills of its manpower (Rush et al. 2001). On studying

Spanish automobiles and textiles, Mamkoottam and Herbolzeimer (1990 and 1991) found that the absence of simultaneous changes can delay, if not totally prevent, the introduction of new technologies. In order to avail themselves of the advantage of what Fleck (1987) terms 'configuration technologies', it is essential for firms to adopt an approach based on 'synchronous innovation', as suggested by Ettlie (1988). The adoption of the new technologies would require a 'paradigm shift', entailing the integration of innovation in products and processes with new ways of designing organizations (Bessant et al., 1990). Such a shift would involve wide-ranging changes in the areas of skills, the organization of work, functional integration, control, interorganizational relationships and the work culture, to mention a few examples. In fact, the changes in these areas have to be coordinated by all the members of the organization. The people would have to first begin believing in a common set of values, then strive unitedly to achieve the mission of the organization. These issues are discussed in some detail in Chapter 4.

Technological Change and Human Resources

The intimate relationship between technology, market dynamics and social institutions is well accepted, but the nature and direction of their linkages are still subject to debate. It is not difficult to identify the areas and extent of the diffusion/application of technology, or the changes in the trends of production and services. It is also quite clear that the pattern of employment, quality of human resources, organizational changes and other variables related to the labour market are interlinked with technological changes. However, it is not easy to establish how far the shifts in these areas can be directly attributed to technological changes/ innovations. This debate has gathered further momentum with the emergence of the new technologies (i.e., those largely based on microelectronics and IT).

Sociologists have used the Durkheimian concept of 'division of labour' to explain the interaction between technological change, on the one hand, and the organization of work, as well as the generation and distribution of skills, on the other. Since Durkheim, industrial sociologists have evolved other views on the relationship between technology and labour. The first view, called the 'decline and rise of skills', was proposed by Woodward (1965). He suggested that the trend of degradation of work roles would be followed by a new trend of upgrading and enrichment. He saw this reversal in trend as part of an evolutionary process, a process which could be attributed to new technology and the growing prevalence of continuous-process production.

Braverman (1974) put forward a different view, which gave a new direction to the ongoing debate. According to his theory, the degradation of work and polarization of skills resulted from the implementation of new technology. The major focus of the discussion now shifted to the consequences of the process applications of microelectronics. Braverman propounded a second view, known as the *degradation of work* or *polarization of skills*. He proposed that in capitalist production, complex work roles are continuously broken up and divided in two ways. They may be broken up into (*a*) lower grade, more routine, simple and monotonous roles, within a relatively segmented organization of work-flow; and (*b*) more demanding, responsible and varied roles, based on better education and training.

Both approaches are based on a deterministic view of technological change and work. A third approach, which stressed the importance of *socio-technical choice*, was put forward on the basis of research at the Tavistock Institute. According to it, the evolution of work is in no way determined by the course of technological change. Instead, it is determined by the choices of the organization's key decision-makers in the sphere of strategy. This view suggests that the development of the technical, social and sentient systems of an organization should be founded on a strategy of enriching skills and achieving an overlapping, rather than divisive, organization of tasks. On the basis of the results of their work on the applications of microelectronics, researchers like Sorge et al. (1988), Kern and Schumann (1987), and Hyman and Streeck (1988) decided to subscribe to the third view.

Post-modern industrial society is distinguished by the predominance of information technology, on the one hand, and the prevalence of the application of management methods and principles, on the other. The enormous amount of attention paid by scholars and practitioners, in recent years, to the field of management has contributed to the development of new ways of manufacturing and marketing products and services, as well as new ways of managing people, finances and the organization. Information technology, in particular, has had the most serious impact on management philosophy and systems. Due to the unprecedented competitiveness of the modern (globalized) market, the supreme focus has come to lie on the concepts of quality, design and flexibility. While these developments have had an immense impact on the occupational structure, the composition of skills, the structure of the organization, communication systems, trade union density and the quality of working life, they have, at the same time, been guided and controlled by the latter.

New technology is almost always equated with IT and its applications. In fact, a major part of the activities of modern organizations, whether in the sphere of manufacturing or services, is based on the application of computers and their convergence with communication technologies. The potential of using a technology which offers dramatic improvements in the way we manage our information activities is highly significant. Unlike earlier technologies, which are specific to a particular process or area in manufacturing, IT is seen as a pervasive and integrative technology. It offers significant improvements across a wide range of activities, as well as in quality and flexibility. The new technology can serve as a powerful weapon for formulating superior strategies, which would place an organization in a better position to achieve its long-term goals.

Flexibility

Flexibility is central to the functioning of modern business and industry. It is an all-pervasive concept, covering the designing and manufacturing of products, the production process and labour. Flexibility in the sphere of labour refers to a variety of decisions affecting the geographical distribution of and occupational changes among the workers, besides their recruitment, deployment and working hours. If a firm is flexibile, it can modify its course of action in accordance with a sudden, unexpected situation. Central to the notion of flexibility is the capability of a system to generate a variety of options, so that things can be done differently or another option can be tried if need be. Flexibility, thus, allows for versatility and resilience—qualities which modern industry must possess. Flexibility is also required for coping with fluctuations in market demand, which may vary wildly in response to changing tastes, seasonal demands, advertising and other variables. An inability to meet market demand and the customer's needs can damage the viability of a business.

Customers want reliable products, easy availability of products, and rapid response in terms of sales and after-sales services. A higher degree of flexibility is required also in the scheduling of work and in the routine within the work place/organization itself. Further, greater flexibility would allow for a more efficient use of the capital invested in the plants, equipment, infrastructure and human resources. These could then be used for producing a greater variety of products/services. Organizations have been moving towards greater flexibility by reducing the volume of production and enhancing the degree of specialization and customization.

Atkinson (1984) identified three different aspects of a flexible firm: (*a*) *functional flexibility*, (*b*) *numerical flexibility*, and (*c*) *financial flexibility*. Financial flexibility refers to the ease with which the tasks performed by the employees can be adjusted to meet changes in the market and in technology, or other contingencies. A variety of skills among the workers would make the challenge of meeting contingencies easier. Numerical flexibility refers to the ease with which the number of employees can be adjusted to meet fluctuations in demand, or other contingencies. There has been a trend towards operating with a core workforce in addition to a peripheral one. The core workforce remains the main and permanent force, while the peripheral one is retained and recalled for shorter periods, on part-time and contractual basis. Financial flexibility refers to the extent to which the structure of pay encourages and supports numerical and functional flexibility. This entails less rigid payment systems, which can motivate individuals to perform better and reward them accordingly.

The need for greater flexibility questions some of the basic principles of traditional (production) work organizations, which have been based on rigid systems and elaborate division of labour. These issues are discussed in Chapters 4 and 5, with particular reference to the Indian context.

Occupational Structure and Skills

The relationship between technology, the occupational structure and the employees' skills is a complex one. While obsolete knowledge and skills can act as constraints in the adoption of new technology, the latter may facilitate the development of new knowledge and skills. As Campbell (1992) observes, high levels of technological change will be increasingly associated with hybrid (or mixed) skills. This implies a scenario in which the workers and managers have less specialized training and a broader range of newly acquired capabilities to cope with the emerging technological challenges. Low levels of technological change may be associated with low levels of skill. By far, the most serious concern is the development of suitable skills and expertise to support the application of new technology. In general, IT poses a number of challenges in the sphere of the acquisition of broader skills. These entail giving direct support to the adoption of IT, and supervising and managing systems based around it. Some examples are the development of skills in systems analysis and programming to find new applications, skills in maintaining and testing microelectronics, and skills in managing the increased flow of information made available to organizations.

The new trend represents a shift from operating skills to those of designing, programming and analysis, maintenance, diagnosis and supervision. This pattern has resulted in a decline in the number of employees and higher levels of skill. In some countries, this trend has created serious problems, as there may not be enough skilled people available to support a microelectronics-based system. Even developed nations, such as Germany, do not have adequate numbers of IT professionals. Countries like Japan and the Republic of Korea have invested heavily in the development of appropriate skills and, therefore, do not face such problems. Further, the range of the skills required is expanding. There is a major requirement for core skills, as also for an increasing convergence of skills. It must also be stressed that higher levels of skill are required not just at the level of operators and those responsible for maintenance, but also at the managerial level. The absence of such skills at the managerial level could limit a firm's ability to exploit new technology to maximum advantage, as indicated by the cases of some developing countries, in particular. Chapter 4 outlines two case studies of this type.

As products are customized using flexible technology, the ways in which machines are used affects the occupational profile of the workplace. Better skilled operators, backed up by highly trained technicians and engineers, become more predominant in the new workplace. According to Schumann (1990), a holistic approach with reduced division of labour is proving to be more efficient than the traditional 'Tayloristic rationalization' patterns (quoted in Campbell, 1992). Studies of the British engineering industry (Henderson, 1989; Senker and Beesley, 1986) show how technological changes alter the occupational structure in favour of the highly skilled strata. Fewer people need to be employed in manufacturing, and they form the 'white-coat' labour forces. A mushroom-shaped organizational profile seems to be replacing the traditional pyramidal structure. In the new set-up, a small number of managers direct a much larger number of engineers, who are supported by a much smaller number of technicians and a diminishing number of other ranks of employees.

The miniaturization and automation of microelectronics is gradually displacing the familiar labour-intensive operations. Campbell and Warner (1992) suggest that the changes required in the mix of skills are likely to alter the nature of the workforce in the following two ways. First, employees with distinctly new skills will be represented in the workplace. Second, since many workers will have acquired several new skills together with their existing ones, there will be a *hybridization* of skills. Thus, the application of microelectronics seems to be reversing the trend associated with industrialization and technological change in the past, when the requirement was for a higher degree of specialization of functions. The craftsman trained in a single discipline has no foreseeable future, and the shift is in favour of the multi-skilled professional worker.

Workers are now expected to co-operate across occupational boundaries. They are required to have theoretical knowledge in a range of fields, matched by practical experience and diagnostic skills. This type of co-operation and mix of skills in the workplace enable the workers to cope with a greater variety of tasks across different and related functions, such as production and maintenance. Functioning effectively with the new technologies entails a growing blend between the skills of the operator and those required for maintenance. Reports from the fieldwork of a large electronics firm, which makes information technology equipment, show that in the UK the employees may learn a wider range of less narrow skills, and/or more or fewer specialized ones (Campbell and Warner 1992). Maintenance craftsmen may need to acquire more engineering and electrical skills, as well as some new skills in the field of electronic technology. Mamkoottam and Herbolzeimer (1991) have observed similar developments in automobile and textile companies in Spain.

The new technologies have thus affected the structure of employment and the requirement of skills at work. Howell and Wolf (1991) differentiated skills into three categories—(*a*) cognitive, (*b*) interactive, and (*c*) motor skills. They noticed a decline in the growth of cognitive skills, and a slight decline in the rate of growth of interactive skills from the 1960s to the 1970s among the professional, technical and managerial staff. They also observed that the growth of the level of cognitive skills was faster for non-supervisory workers than for supervisory workers. On the other hand, interactive skills grew substantially faster in the supervisory category. This shift has been attributed to the introduction of new technologies, which have reduced the need for jobs that require low cognitive skills in the manufacturing sector. The same reason can be cited for the relatively rapid growth in the average level of cognitive skills among the non-supervisory occupations. In other words, the new technology requires teamwork, inter-functional coordination and integration.

The rapid growth of IT and Internet-based knowledge economy have led to a quantum jump in the value of cognitive skills. Burton-Jones (1999) argues that knowledge is transforming the nature of production and consequently, that of work, jobs, the firm, the

market and every aspect of economic activity. These issues are
discussed with special reference to the Indian context in Chapters 3 and 5.

Technological Change and the (New) Worker

The integrative nature of the new technology requires increasing
competence across a range of traditional and new disciplines.
The maintenance of industrial robots, for example, requires skills
in microelectronics, in electrical and mechanical engineering,
hydraulics, pneumatics, as well as diagnostic and system analysis. The trend among the process industries, banking and finance,
the food processing and electronics industries, engineering and
services, shows a greater integration of tasks, besides a need for
'cross-trading' and a demand for multi-skilled workers. The new
worker must not only possess a higher degree of technical knowledge, but should also be more adaptable to new situations. He should
be able to respond quickly to technical problems, and should be
ready to work as part of a team. The traditional qualifications of
physical strength and individual work ability no longer suffice.

The new technology calls for a polyvalent and professional
worker, who should not only understand the basic process of production, but should also have some knowledge of the functioning and operation of the new machines. As these machines are
flexible and versatile, they require these very qualities from the
new employee. The employee must be conceptually and techni-
cally competent. He should be open-minded, and willing to learn
and co-operate with others. Thus, in a sense, he is expected to
function like a 'superman'.

The new polyvalent worker performs a larger number of tasks.
He occupies positions encompassing broader job descriptions. He
works within a less hierarchical framework, in which the division of labour is less marked. In general, this is reflected in the
overall reduction in the number of employees required to perform a given set of operations. This trend would be more prominent at the levels of the unskilled and semi-skilled workers, as
their jobs are easily mechanized and they can be replaced by

machines. The three traditional categories of unskilled, semi-skilled and skilled workers are being replaced by two categories, consisting of less skilled and highly skilled workers. The number of workers belonging to the unskilled category would gradually decline, and this group would eventually be eliminated and merged with the group of less skilled workers. At the same time, the numbers in the skilled category would grow in size and importance. This increase would spur on further changes in the structure of the organization. In fact, the IT industry, which employs mostly knowledge workers, is already experiencing the need for a new organizational structure (a virtual organization!).

The experience of the developed economies, which shows a greater demand for professional engineers, technicians and professional managers, is also reflected in the changes in the educational aspirations of individuals today. People are becoming more conscious of the need for higher levels of qualification, and they aim for greater personal development. There is a greater emphasis on flexibility and creative problem-solving skills. Also, the stress is on understanding and appreciating the whole system, rather than a small part of it. There is a body of research showing a trend towards cross-trading, as well as continuous education and training, to update skills in order to fight the ever-faster rate of obsolescence.

Training and continuous education are a must because in the emerging pattern, skills often have a short life cycle, and the ability to acquire new skills and update old ones becomes critical for one's professional survival. This, in turn, shifts the focus from task-related training to personal development. Tacit knowledge and ability have, thus, assumed greater importance, so that many firms are starting to recognize the advantages of becoming a 'learning organization'. Chapter 4 discusses the developments in these areas, with reference to the Indian context.

Major changes are taking place in the composition of the workforce, in terms of gender, age and educational qualifications, across the world. An increasing number of women are entering the work-force, especially in the developing countries, where relatively few women have been absorbed so far. William Johnston (1991) has observed that the trend of women leaving home-based employment to enter the paid workforce is a demographic reality of industrialization that is often overlooked. Women are likely to be absorbed increasingly into the industrial sector as cooking and cleaning technology ease the burden at home, agricultural jobs diminish, and other jobs—especially in the service sector—proliferate. More than half of all women between the ages of 15 and 64 are now estimated to work outside the home; and women comprise nearly one-third of the world's organized workforce. However, the developed economies have absorbed many more women into the labour force than have the developing economies. Women in the Scandinavian countries are reported to hold more than 50 per cent of the jobs available.

A larger presence of women at the workplace will have an influence on the working conditions and terms of employment. It may also create demands for new services, such as the provision of fast food, day care for children, home-cleaning services and nursing homes. More importantly, since the home places more demands on women than on men, women are likely to be away from work more often than men. For this reason, the time schedule at the workplace may have to be restructured to allow for greater flexibility and other innovative methods of deployment.

Technology and Organizational Change

Studies show that the full benefits of new technologies can be derived only if simultaneous changes are brought about in the organization's structure, physical layout, manpower skills and the work culture. The case of Spanish automobiles and textiles has already been cited in this context. It is generally accepted that technological change requires, and also results in, organizational change. The innovation theory suggests that compatibility, i.e., the degree to which an innovation fits into the context it is being placed in, is an important determinant of the success of the technology adopted. This is particularly true in the case of a changeover to new technology. Many commentators have spoken of the need for 'a new way of thinking', as the adoption of new technologies requires a 'paradigm shift'. This shift entails the integration of production and process innovations along with new patterns of organizational design (Bessant, 1993).

Technological change requires the organization to go beyond its normal learning curve. New and radically extended answers have to be found to cope with the multi-dimensional changes, which affect every aspect of the organization. This process often requires an element of 'unlearning' and 'creative destruction'. Organizational change is not an automatic consequence of the introduction of new technology, and has to be initiated deliberately and implemented effectively. The changes have to be introduced at the individual, group and interfunctional levels, and at the level of the organization. The traditional model of (work) organization based on 'Fordism' is giving way to the new model of 'Toyotism', bringing about major changes in the areas of skills, work organization, functional integration, control, inter-organizational relationships and organizational culture. In the absence of one 'best choice' in any of these areas, and given the possibility of various contingencies, organizations are expected to make their own choices regarding strategy. As Child (1977) suggested, these choices have to be made in the context of the given environmental contingencies, technologies and structure of the organization. Needless to say, the choices made in today's increasingly uncertain world demand a high level of flexibility from the organization. The Indian experience in this context is briefly dealt with in Chapter 4.

Technology may be seen essentially as a system involving both tools and organization around the use of those tools. Technology should be seen and managed as a total system and appropriate attention must be paid to the organizational dimensions. We have already mentioned several of the changes that an organization would have to introduce to cope with the unpredictable environment and new technology. These include the need for greater flexibility, greater co-operation among the employees, and the development of various skills, especially those related to the rapid processing of information and decision making.

In order to be able to respond quickly to unexpected challenges, the organization should encourage local autonomy and decentralized decision making, which allow for a fair degree of functional flexibility. The highly interdependent systems, designed to deal with high levels of uncertainty and local diversity, require decentralization of control to the operating point at the local levels. It is argued that flexible response can be offered through a combination of flexible technology and flexible organization. Further, the workers should be given a broad task specification, within which they would be expected to organize themselves by allocating roles, scheduling tasks, and so on.

According to Bessant (1993), the greater degree of functional flexibility and integration create 'a factory within the factory', giving rise to many specialized roles within the same organization. The increasing technological integration forces functional groups to work more closely together. For example, CAD and CAM require a much closer relationship between design and manufacturing. Similarly, in order to maintain quality standards, a close relationship is required between production, maintenance and quality control.

Organizational Culture

It is often held that technological change entails a paradigm shift, and all paradigm shifts involve values and norms. The introduction/implementation of technological innovations would become very difficult, if not impossible, in the absence of a shift in the organization's culture. All technologies may be seen to be couched in a 'way of thinking'. According to Burns and Stalker (1961), it is the 'organic' type of organization, as against the 'mechanistic' one, which is better equipped to accept technological changes. Organic organizations encourage innovation, lateral rather than vertical communication, a higher degree of decentralization, flexibility and integration. According to Child (1977) and Handy (1980), organizational change is possible only if all the members within an organization share the same values and goals. Such commitment can be ensured if the workers feel a sense of ownership and participation/involvement. This runs counter to the traditional model of organizations, in which the worker is at the periphery.

However, it may also be observed that the options available for the design of a work organization depend on the skills available within it. There would be more options available to an organization, which has promoted a higher level of skills, as well as training to support multi-functionality. The Scandinavian countries and Japan have conducted more experiments in teamwork and the use of multi-skilled workers than have countries like the UK and the US. This is because the relative levels of skill in the latter are much lower and are distributed more narrowly across the workforce (Senker, 1990; Rush and Bessant, 1989). These issues are discussed with reference to the Indian context in Chapters 4 and 6.

Quality of Work Life

The physical and the socio-psychological implications of the new technology are not without ambiguities and contradictions. While the new worker has to be better skilled, must perform a job entailing more responsibilities than his earlier counterpart, and is under greater stress, his wages may not always be enhanced correspondingly. This is more so as often, the worker may not be given a promotion despite the fact that he has acquired new or higher skills, and his job classification may remain just the same. In fact, trade unions have argued that the introduction of new technology often leads to a fall in the real wages of the employees. A study covering a number of new technology agreements in the UK during 1979–80 showed that the unions often secured agreements which guaranteed that their earnings would not be reduced and that those who were redeployed would not be downgraded. However, the unions seldom secured an increase in the earnings of those operating the new technology (Manwarring, 1981). Mamkoottam and Herbolzeimer (1990) report similar findings from their study of the automobile and textile sectors in Spain. Chapter 5 discusses this aspect with reference to the Indian context.

Human skills are increasingly being incorporated into machines, which automatically perform many simultaneous and sophisticated functions with the help of microprocessors and electronic data processing applications. In this process, the worker is bound to become increasingly subservient to the machine, his job being mainly to assist and maintain the machine to help it perform the major operations. Robotics, as well as the incorporation of microelectronics in the manufacturing and service functions, show us how machines control the worker, setting the process and pace of work. This necessarily increases the monotony of the worker's job. It also increases his sense of isolation because often, a single worker manages a whole unit of automated processes.

In the context of new technology, the worker receives less direct supervision and thus, enjoys greater autonomy than earlier. At the same time, however, machines impose a greater control on him, which immediately reduces the area of his freedom. Moreover, as the rate of technological change grows, workers in general, and those in the older age groups in particular, find it extremely difficult to retain themselves in the face of the faster rate of (technological) obsolescence. Similarly, though new technology often results in an improvement in the work environment and conditions, reducing the level of dust, dirt, noise and physical strain, it also raises the level of psychological stress of the worker. Although teamwork, job rotation, group tasks and schemes for employee involvement are meant to mitigate these evils, they have yet to become a popular practice in most cases, including India.

Employment

The extent to which globalization and liberalization have helped the national economies, especially in terms of their impact on the employment situation, has, indeed, become debatable. The recent trends in unemployment are particularly disturbing. Despite a steady improvement in the world economy, open unemployment has grown in most countries. This new phenomenon, which has characterized the years since the 1990s, has been termed 'jobless growth.' The growth in employment has lagged behind that of both output and the labour force. In the OECD countries, the GDP was expected to grow from a base of 100 in 1975 to 191 by the year 2000, while employment was expected to grow from a base of 100 to only 124 in the same period. The corresponding figures for south Asia for the same period were 100 to 299 and

100 to only 154, respectively. In East Asia, the GDP was expected to grow by more than five times, and employment from a base of 100 to only 155 in the same period.

Similarly, a widening gap is projected in terms of the growth in the labour force and in employment. In the OECD countries, the labour force was expected to grow from a base of 100 in 1990 to 105 by the year 2000, and employment from 100 to 104 in the same period. The situation was projected to be much worse in South Asia, where the labour force was expected to grow from 100 to 122, and employment only up to 116, in the same period. In East Asia, the labour force was expected to grow up to 137 and employment up to 117 by the year 2000.

In the case of India, there is an increasing gap between the growth in population and the growth rate of employment. While the number of workers in the total population increased by 26.8 per cent during 1981–1991, the rate of employment between 1977–78 and 1987–88 grew only by 1.95 per cent, which means an all-India unemployment rate of 3.77 (Ministry of Labour, 1994–95). In fact, demographic factors are likely to exert an additional pressure on the employment scenario in India. The proportion of the dependent age-group (between the ages of 0–14 years) to the total population will decline, while the proportions of people in the age-groups of 15–64 and 65 years and above are expected to increase substantially in the coming years. These demographic changes will, no doubt, aggravate the unemployment problem.

Many argue that in the Indian context, liberalization has adversely affected the employment rate. However, others suggest that the overall employment rate has improved since 1991, compared to the pre-reform period. On the basis of various empirical data, Dev (2000) argues that liberalization policies are likely to have a significant impact on the employment and incomes of the poor of South Asia. According to him, the macro-level picture can be misleading and the micro-level realities indicate a decline in the rate of employment in the organized sector. On the other hand, Goldar (2000) refutes the pessimistic position taken by most studies and argues that employment in the organized manufacturing sector in India was stagnant during the 1980s, but grew in the 1990s. Analyzing the Annual Survey of Industries (ASI) data,

Goldar further suggests that this growth was due to the change in the size structure of industries in favour of small and medium-scale industries, as well as the slow-down in the growth of real wages—factors facilitated as a result of liberalization. During the pre-reform decade, employment in the high-productivity factory-manufacturing segment increased at the rate of 0.53 per cent per annum, in response to a higher growth rate of 8.7 per cent in manufacturing output. Though the growth in the latter came down to 7.4 per cent per annum during the post-reform period, that in employment rose by 2.7 per cent annually. Unlike the pre-reform decade, when employment in the public sector grew at more than double the average rate, the growth rate of employment in the private factory-manufacturing segment was above average in the post-reform period.

According to Goldar, the policy regime of the post-reform period had a major influence on the size structure of industries. In the early 1960s, factory employment was heavily concentrated in very large establishments. Small establishments were at a disadvantage due to the policies pertaining to protection, investment incentives and credit control, as well as the promotion of public-sector industries. Since the imbalance in the size structure was largely a consequence of economic policies, the correction that has taken place in the last two decades may be attributed, at least in part, to changes in the economic policy, especially the liberalization of the industrial and trade policies (Goldar 2000). This change in the size structure would naturally have had an impact on the occupational structure as well.

K. Sundaram (2000) made an analysis of the growth of population and the structure of occupations. He found that the share of the trade, hotels and restaurants sector alone had risen by 33 points, while that of the services sector (excluding construction), taken as a whole, had increased from 124 per 1000 in 1961 to 203 per 1000 in 1993–94 (by 79 points). Thus, it was largely the tertiary sector, rather than the secondary sector, which benefited from the decline in the share of agriculture and allied activities in the aggregate workforce. According to Sundaram, an overwhelming proportion of the additions to the workforce in the manufacturing and repair services sectors has been absorbed by the low-productivity, unorganized manufacturing establishments. It may be noted that during the same period, though the unregistered manufacturing sector absorbed 83 per cent of the incremental workforce, it accounted for only 34 per cent of the incremental GDP originating in the manufacturing sector. This indicates the failure of the high-productivity organized manufacturing sector to absorb the large increases in the workforce, increases generated by the population growth in India. It is also widely recognized that in the post-globalized world and the liberalized India, the informal sector has been growing rapidly and the formal sector has been shrinking drastically. This may be attributed, in large part, to the slow or delayed introduction of technological innovations in the large-scale manufacturing industry.

T. S. Papola (1989) observes that labour-saving technological changes have taken place in practically all branches of Indian industry. In industries and units in which technological changes have been rapid and significant, the employment potential has declined. However, employment is declining also in the older industries, in which technological change was delayed or slow, due to stagnation in output. One can, therefore, make the interesting observation that regardless of whether technological change has been introduced or not, the overall effect on the generation of employment has been adverse.

While it is true that new technology incorporates human skills and manual labour into machines and, thereby, reduces and replaces human labour, it may also be observed that more and more of the new jobs available in the services and manufacturing sectors are in the area of new technology. In other words, there are also new employment opportunities, which may be filled either by those de-skilled and displaced from traditional activities, or by newer entrants. So the question of whether or not microelectronics poses a problem regarding the availability of skills depends on the choices made in the areas of education and training. The general trends in the changes demanded by microelectronics in the sphere of skills are towards higher levels, wider breadth and greater flexibility. These trends may also be responsible for a shift in the relationship between individual workers and the firm. Talking about the increasing role of knowledge workers, Burton-Jones

(1999) suggests that some individuals are likely to form stronger relationships with the firms for which they work, while others are likely to move towards increasingly distant, market-like contractual relationships. Such fundamental changes will result in profound alteration of both the nature of employment and its future role within an organization.

Subcontracting

In response to technological changes, organizations have been developing a two-tier, segmented labour force. The workforce often consists of a group of flexible and multi-skilled workers, who are clustered around a stable core functioning as the permanent force, and another group of workers who are hired on a contractual and temporary basis. The latter are at the periphery. As the market expands, the periphery grows to take up the slack; as growth slows down, the periphery contracts. Those at the periphery consist of subcontracted part-time workers, the self-employed and several others falling in the category of casual, home-based temporary workers. Their wages are comparatively lower and their contracts are more short-term. They are neither protected by labour laws, nor organized by the trade unions, and are, thus, bereft of the benefits available to permanent employees. Though subcontracting always existed, it appears to increase with the introduction of new technology. Therefore, the indication is that the trend of subcontracting will continue, and perhaps increase. Although the trade unions have been trying to restrain the management from subcontracting jobs, the new tendency towards what is commonly referred to as 'neo-liberal flexibilization', and its legitimization by state legislation will make subcontracting more popular and easier. A growth in subcontracting, in turn, leads to a higher level of labour segmentation. More and more jobs will be removed from the core sector to the peripheral (informal) sector, which will become less secure and more isolated from the external labour market and the wider protection afforded by trade unions.

Papola (1989) observes that the growth of employment in India has been widely divergent, and the real explanation for this fact lies in the practice of subcontracting. Conditions have become favourable for large-scale subcontracting. A large number of small units have come up in recent years, particularly in the manufacturing sector, and these are not in a position to compete with the larger units with brand names and high market shares. In fact, the small units produce for the larger units, and the latter find it economical to use the capacity of the former. As the expenditure on wages is usually much lower in the smaller units, the parent firm avoids the problems associated with the management of a large workforce. These problems include the management of industrial relations, and the payment of post-retirement and other benefits. The wages paid in the small units usually amount to about two-thirds of those paid in the large units. Further, subcontracted units are not provided with social security and other benefits. Subcontracting is widespread in almost all sectors. According to an estimate, not more than 40 per cent of the production is undertaken in the parent unit. All these issues directly or indirectly concern the trade unions as well.

Globalization and Trade Unions

Trade unions are a product of industrialized society and have played an important role in modern times. Since the trade union movement started, trade unions have not only grown geographically across the world, but have also assumed a more important role. This has happened in different ways in different countries, and at different points in history. These particulars have affected the structural and political (i.e., strategy-related) dimensions of trade unions in various ways. Over the years, trade unions have responded to the changing environment by redefining their role and strategy. The craft-based structure of the unions of the initial years gave way to industrial unions, which developed centralized power/bargaining centres at the national or sectoral levels. In the US and UK, it was the centralized and conflict-oriented model of collective bargaining and industrial relations that developed. In West Germany and Japan of the post-World War II period, industrial relations took a decentralized and co-operative form. In the post-war era, the modern structures for labour and management co-operation have been influenced by the economic and social environments of the countries or regions to which they be-long. In Japan, such co-operation was built on the presence of 'quasi-communities of labour', which adopted a problem-solving approach within enterprises. The quasi-communities helped develop a pattern for the restructuring of enterprises, and encouraged flexible employment practices. These practices were based on the retraining and relocation of workers, with a minimum of lay-offs. The Works Councils, which started in countries like Germany, where labour and business practise mutually beneficial consultation, are now being adopted all over Europe (Jose, 2000).

As mentioned earlier, the past few decades have witnessed enormous changes in the political and economic environment. These changes are, perhaps, unprecedented in dimension and intensity. The globalization of national economies and the internationalization of products and services have brought about paradigmatic changes in product, marketing and labour (human resource management) strategies. Consequently, labour–capital–management relations have also had to be realigned. International competition and technological innovation have resulted in new ways of organizing capital and other resources. Policies relating to the labour market have had to become more flexible and constant innovation has become a must, due to the presence of new products with shorter life cycles. An additional factor in this context is today's demand (consumer)-driven market, which has become highly price (cost)-sensitive and quality-sensitive. Innovative forms of organizing work and a new generation of employees, with a different composition of skills and career aspirations, may be seen as natural corollaries of the recent developments. Above all, the role of the state and the relevance of public sector enterprises have become an issue of contention in most parts of the world, including the erstwhile Soviet Union.

The importance of trade unions has receded and their membership has declined in recent decades, due to the new work environment. This decline and the associated 'crisis of representation' have become a subject of debate for a decade or more. There is a lot of speculation on the future of trade unions. Upchurch et al. (2000), on the one hand, refer to the pessimistic conclusions of Valkenburg (1996) and Phelps-Brown (1992), who associate the growing individualism of the worker and the fragmentation of the working class with the decline of trade unionism as a 'solidaristic' movement. On the other hand, they suggest that there is a substantial body of empirical evidence to contradict such conclusions. They refer to the works of Lind (1996) in Denmark and Waddington and Whitson (1997) in the UK, which show no such evidence indicating a shift from collectivism to individualism. Upchurch et al. argue that many of the traditional values of trade unionism—job security, full employment, fair distribution of wealth, democracy at work—are precisely the principles that have been denigrated by the new employer offensive. This raises the question of the structure and strategy that trade unions may have to adopt to successfully mobilize membership and survive in the not-so-favourable, if not hostile, climate.

In sum, globalization, in general, and technological change, in particular, have had a colossal impact on the labour and human resource dimensions of the modern workplace. The higher levels of quality, flexibility and cost-efficiency in today's competitive environment are leading to major changes in work processes, the organization of work, and the kind of knowledge and skills required of the workers and managers. Moreover, globalization and technological change have brought about radical changes in the conditions prevailing in the labour market; organizational culture; and the way the workplace is managed, including trade unions and industrial relations.

References

Atkinson, J. (1984). *The Flexible Firm*. Sussex: Institute of Manpower Studies, Sussex University.

Bessant, J. (1993). 'Towards Factory 2000: Design Organizations for Computer-integrated technologies'. In J. Clark (ed.), *Human Resource Management and Technological Change*. London: Sage Publications.

Bessant, J. Levy, P., Ley, C., Smith, S. and **Tranfield, D.** (1990). *Management and Organization for Computer-integrated Technologies*. Brighton: Centre for Business Research, Brighton Polytechnic.

Braverman, H. (1974). *Labour and Monopoly Capital*. New York: Monthly Review.

Burns, T. and **Stalker, G. M.** (1961). *The Management of Innovation*. London, Tavistock.

Burton-Jones, A. (1999). *Knowledge Capitalism.* Oxford, New York: Oxford University Press.

Campbell, A. and **Warner, M.** (1992). *New Technology, Skills and Management,* London: Routledge.

Child, J. (1977). *Organization: A Guide to problems and Practices.* London, Harper and Row,

Daniel, W. W. and **Millward, N.** (1993). 'Workplace industrial relations'. In J. Clark (ed.), *Human resource management and Technical change.* London: Sage Publications.

Dev, S. Mohan (2000). 'Economic liberalization and employment in South Asia'. *Economic and Political Weekly,* January 8: pp. 40–51.

Ettlie, J. (1988). *Taking Charge of Manufacturing.* San Francisco: Jossey–Bass.

Fleck, J. (1987). Innofusion or diffuzation? Working paper, University of Edinburgh, Department of Business Studies.

Goldar, B. (2000). Employment growth in organised manufacturing in India. *Economic and Political Weekly,* April 1: vol. xxxv. No. 14, pp. 1191–1195.

Henderson, J. (1989). *The Globalization of High Technology of Production,* London: Routledge.

Hyman, R. and **Seeck. W.** (1988). *New Technology and Industrial Relations.* New York: Basil Blackwell.

Johnston, W. (1991). 'Global workforce 2000: The new world labour market'. *Harvard Business Review,* March-April, pp. 115–127.

Jose, A. V. (2000). The future of the labour movement: Some observations on developing countries. Discussion paper presented at the Labour and Society Programme, International Institute of Labour Studies, Geneva.

Kern, H. and **Schumann, M.** (1987). 'Limits of the division of labour'. *Economic and Industrial Democracy,* vol. 8, no. 2: pp. 151–170.

Lind, J. (1996). 'Trade unions: Social movement or welfare apparatus'? *Capital and Class,* 65, pp. 9–20.

Mamkoottam, K. (1994). 'Globalization and the emerging labour–management relations'. In C.S. Venkata Ratnam et al. (eds), *Labour and Unions in a Period of Transition.* New Delhi: Friedrich Ebert Stiftung.

Mamkoottam, K. and **Herbolzeimer, E.** (1990). Interface of new technology and human resource management: A case of automobiles and textiles in Spain. Report published by the European Foundation for Management Development (EFMD).

Mamkootam, K. and **Herbolzeimer, E.** (1991). 'Human resource implications of new technology: A case study of automobiles in Spain'. *Indian Journal of Industrial Relations,* 26(3): pp. 205–226.

Manwarring, T. (1981). 'The trade union response to new technology'. *Industrial Relations Journal,* vol. 12, no. 4, pp. 7–26.

Marshall, R. (1992). 'The future role of government in industrial relations'. In M.F. Bognanno and M.M. Kleiner (eds), *Labour Market Institutions and the Future Role of Unions.* Massachusetts: Blackwell.

Ministry of Labour (1995). Annual Report, 1994–95. New Delhi: Government of India.

Papola, T. S. (1989). 'Restructuring in Indian industry: Implication for Employment and industrial relations'. In G. Edgren (ed), *Restructuring Employment and Industrial Relations*, Geneva Asian Regional Team for Employment Promotion, ILO.

Phelps-Brown, H. (1992). 'The counter-revolution of our time'. *Industrial Relations*, 29(1)' pp. 1–14.

Porter, M. (1990). *Competitive Advantage of Nations*. New York: Free Press.

Rush, H. and **Bessant, J.** (2001). Revolution in three-quarters time: Lessons from the diffusion of advanced manufacturing technologies. Brighton: Centre for Business Research, Brighton Polytechnic.

Schumann, M. (1990). 'Changing concepts of work and qualifications'. In M. Warner et al. (eds) *New Technology and Manufacturing Management*. London ,Wiley.

Senker, P. and **Beesley, M.** (1986). 'The need for skills in the factory of the Future'. *New Technology, Work and Employment*, vol. 1, no. 1, pp. 9–17.

Sorge, A. and **Streeck, W.** (1988). 'Industrial relations and technical change'. In Hyman, R. and Streeck, W. *New Technology and Industrial Relations*. New York, Basil Blackwell.

Sundaram, K. (2000). Economic development: Employment and occupational diversification. New Delhi: Paper presented at the Millennium Conference on Population, Development and Environment Nexus, February, pg. 14–16.

Upchurch, M., **Danford, A.** and **Richardson, M.** (2000). Trade union response to industrial restructuring: Sectoral case studies from the southwest of England. Paper presented at the Fourth International Progressive Policy Congress Hamburg, March 2–5.

Valkenburg, B. (1996). 'Individualization and solidarity: The challenge of modernization'. In P. Leisink et al. (eds), *The Challenge to Trade Unions in Europe*. Cheltenham: Edward Elgar.

Waddington, J. and **Whitson, C.** (1997). 'Why do people join unions in a period of membership decline'? In *Journal of Industrial Relations*, 354: pp. 515–46.

Willman, P. (1986). *Technological Change, Collective Bargaining and Industrial Efficiency*. Oxford: Clarendon Press.

Womack, J.P., **Jones, D.T.** and **Roos, D.** (1990). *The Machine that Changed the World*. New York: Maxwell Macmillan, International.

Woodward, J. (1965). *Industrial Organization: Theory and Practice*. Oxford: Oxford University Press.

World Bank (1995). *The World Development Report, 1995*. New York: The World Bank.

3

Structural Changes and Labour in India

Introduction

In the recent past, economies across the world have experienced structural changes of different magnitudes. While some of these changes may have been proactive in nature, others have been reactive. In fact, it appears that we are living through one of those infrequent periods in history when we are overtaken by profound changes, which are unprecedented in their direction, speed and intensity. As mentioned earlier, given the nature of the new technology that has to be introduced, the absence of a simultaneous approach for restructuring the larger economy, society and the workplace can delay, if not prevent, the introduction of the new technology. Rapid technological developments and globalization left nations and economies across the world with little choice but to compete in the emerging single (world) market. In most countries, restrictions on the movement of capital, goods and services were gradually lifted. Further, global standards came to control quality, price and productivity. With reference to the Indian industrial and financial sectors, structural adjustments and economic reforms were (and continue to be) introduced in order to take advantage of globalization and technological changes.

The New Economic Policy

For several decades after Independence, the Government of India followed a path of industrial development, which placed a major emphasis on the state-owned public sector. The Union and state governments made huge investments of several millions of rupees in the public sector units (PSUs), which controlled the major share in almost every sphere of manufacturing goods and providing services. However, over the years, most of the public sector enterprises became loss-making units and many were declared sick, though we must hasten to add that industrial sickness was by no means confined to the public sector alone. Ironically, industrial sickness was more pervasive in the private sector, particularly in the medium and small-scale units, many of which were taken over by the government. What is more worrying is the fact that several million workers were, and still are, employed in these sick units. Critics attributed the deterioration in the Indian industrial scenario to the unhealthy policy of protectionism, as well as the industry's isolation from the global market. In 1990, *The Economist* used the term 'caged tiger' to describe the over-protected Indian economy. Direct state intervention and bureaucratic control constrained the growth of Indian industry for a long time, be it through industrial licensing, import–export restrictions, or labour legislation. Among the major reasons for the non-competitiveness of Indian industry today are technological obsolescence and the inefficient deployment of manpower. In addition, the skills of the employees are redundant.

In the wake of a severe foreign exchange reserve crisis and the increasing impact of globalization, the Government of India announced a new Industrial Policy in July 1991. The major objective was to transform and integrate the Indian industrial and financial sectors with the global market. The new policy package included several major measures, such as privatization of public sector organizations, modernization and technological change, training of manpower and upgradation of skills, and the rehabilitation of sick industrial units. Most importantly, adequate legislative reforms were introduced to relax state control over industry and finance. An organized effort to tackle industrial sickness had been initiated in 1987 itself, with the enactment of the Sick Industrial Companies (Special Provisions) Act, 1985, and the constitution of the Board of Industrial and Financial Reconstruction (BIFR). The BIFR—a quasi-judicial body—was vested with wide-ranging powers to act as a single window for nursing sick units back to health, or for recommending their closure. Through an amendment to the Sick Industrial Companies Act in 1991, the jurisdiction of BIFR, which was till then confined to private sector units, was enlarged to cover sick public sector units as well.

In countries where free competitive markets have been developed and nurtured over the years, the labour force is entitled to certain unemployment benefits under an overall social security system. Since India had no meaningful social security system, a social safety net was created under the National Renewal Fund (NRF), with the idea of retraining employees and rehabilitating obsolete technology. The main objective of the NRF was to ensure that technological change and the modernization of production processes did not adversely affect the workers. The fund was intended to not only bring in measures to ameliorate the lot of the affected workers, but also to retrain them. This would put them in a position to upgrade their skills so that they could actively participate in the process of change.

As the government attempted to usher in a process of restructuring, technological innovation or modernization, a variety of situations were likely to arise, and the NRF was constituted to deal with three kinds of situations. First, in the case of enterprises that did not need any immediate restructuring but could require it in the foreseeable future, the NRF was to contribute so that adequate funds would be available when the need arose. Second, the NRF would contribute to those units which, though intrinsically viable, needed immediate restructuring. Here, since there could be no opportunity to build up a corpus of funds, the NRF could be used for technological upgradation, restructuring and retraining of labour. However, the units receiving such funds would be expected to undertake a suitable obligation to reimburse the amount, as they became viable over a period of time. Third, the NRF would act as a social safety net for those units which were already sick, and could be referred to the BIFR. The BIFR could order either their closure or revival after making an evaluation. Retrenchment of labour was likely in either case, and the NRF could serve as a funding agency, without obligation of reimbursement. The NRF was structured in accordance with these objectives and was provided with suitable mechanisms to deal with these different situations. However, it has not been very successful in achieving the intended objectives.

As in the case of several other countries, India has not found it easy to traverse the path of change by means of structural reforms in the economy and industry. Structural reforms were introduced by the Indian government amidst a great deal of scepticism among political parties, intellectuals, opinion-makers and bureaucrats within the country. Opinions were divided even among the ministers in the central government. However, the much-fragmented labour unions almost forgot their ideological and historical differences, and came to a common platform to oppose the steps being taken by the government. They were particularly opposed to the restructuring of the public sector. In the absence of political consensus, and faced with widespread protests from organized labour, the then government adopted a cautious approach to reforms. However, it is noteworthy that in the meantime, the economy and industry began to look up. Foreign investment started coming in and a gradual transformation of the Indian corporate sector was under way. Multinationals began to look at India as a profitable sourcing and production centre in several areas, including computer software, cosmetics, garments, heavy engineering, automobiles, airlines and cargo services, potable alcohol, footwear, food chains and cereals. After a decade of reforms, the Indian economy looked healthier, at least in terms of foreign investment, especially foreign direct investment (FDI), in India. On the basis of sources in the RBI, *The Economic Times* (May 27, 2001) reported that on May 18, 2001, foreign investments stood at US $42.829 billion. A healthy proportion of FDI inflows, as compared to portfolio investments, is considered a positive sign, as the former constitute long-term investment. The industrial sector has not only shown a higher growth rate, but has also become more competitive. This is reflected in the growth of exports, a healthy foreign exchange reserve, and growth in employment in the private sector (including the unorganized sector).

It must be noted that the Congress Party, under which the process of liberalization was initiated in early 1991, was voted out of power in the next general elections in 1996. According to many critics, this indicated that the reform process was a political failure.

However, all the subsequent governments and coalitions, whatever their political ideologies, continued with the process of deregulation. They enlarged the areas of foreign and private investment, and the policy of partial privatization (disinvestment) of the public sector has continued. Important sectors, like infrastructure, telecommunications, civil aviation, power and automobiles, have been deregulated and opened to multinational players. Even in the face of nationwide protests and agitation by the employees of the nationalized insurance sector, the Insurance Regulatory and Development Act (IRDA) was passed in the 1999 winter session of Parliament. This act opened up the insurance sector to private/foreign companies. A department of disinvestment, headed by a minister, has been created recently in order to speed up the process of privatization.

The government is considering bringing about changes in the public sector banks too, the idea being to restructure them and gradually open them to disinvestment. The Union Ministry of Finance has directed the banks to draw up a voluntary retirement scheme for the employees in order to increase efficiency. The banks have been asked to reduce their level of operations, and the organizational restructuring is expected to result in major cost-saving. In a recent study by the Federation of Indian Chambers of Commerce and Industry (FICCI), 22 per cent of the staff in 16 nationalized banks were found redundant, when benchmarked on the basis of Rs 125 lakh business per employee (BPE). Steps are being taken to make the public sector undertakings more accountable. Any capital fusion for restructuring plans would be subject to the signing of a Memorandum of Understanding (MOU), in the form of a time-bound schedule for implementation. The schedule will be closely monitored by the ministry to ensure that the PSUs adhere to the conditionalities of the restructuring package. According to sources, the government annually spends about Rs 3000 crore on restructuring plans for various PSUs, in the form of cash, loan write-offs, interest subsidy, and so on. About one-fourth of the 239 PSUs are sick, and the BIFR has declared about 40 as being unfit for revival.

While these steps may have accelerated the reform process, the trade unions and organized labour have tried to apply brakes on the process. Though trade unions and industrial relations have imposed constraints on the liberalization process and associated economic reforms in India, at the same time the reform process, in its turn, has had its own impact on them. As proposed by Dunlop (1958), the nature and climate of industrial relations can be seen as an outcome of the complex set of transactions that take place among the major players, such as the state, employers, employees and trade unions, in a given socio-economic context. Structural reforms and technological innovation affect the environment and thus, industrial relations, directly and in important ways. Technological change and innovation, for example, cannot be considered in isolation from the existing institutional arrangements governing industrial relations. The manner in which the interests of the employers, employees, unions and the wider society are affected by the introduction of technological changes is determined by the interaction between (*a*) the changes made by the different players (government, employers, employees/unions) in the existing human resource management/industrial relations practices, and (*b*) the decisions taken about technological change. To appreciate the exact nature of this symbiotic relationship, we shall now examine the role of the major players in creating the type of industrial relations scenario prevalent in India.

Labour and Industrial Relations in India

Industrial relations should be seen as dynamic in nature. As in most developing countries in the world, the labour movement in India went hand in hand with the country's independence movement. Not only did labour play an active part in the struggle for independence, but the labour movement derived its vitality from the independence movement and sought support from the political leaders. In fact, trade unions continued to be closely linked with political parties in India. After Independence, political parties used organized labour for political purposes, while trade unions found it difficult to succeed and sustain themselves without political patronage. Over the years, the trend towards fragmentation of political parties influenced the nature of trade unionism as well. The various political affiliations divided the labour force into a multiplicity of trade unions. This fragmented trade union structure not only weakened the movement, but also made bilateral negotiation and collective settlements extremely difficult and rare.

Independent India deliberately chose a philosophy of social-ist democracy, which was enshrined within a legislative frame-work, in order to protect the interests of the workers and trade unions. Within this framework, even day-to-day relations between the employer and employee are bound by legislation. Thus, politi-cal parties took it upon themselves to champion the cause of labour. Between the 1950s and 1970s, as the public sector expanded, the number of trade unions kept growing. Moreover, the trade unions became more and more powerful *vis-à-vis* the employers and management, in particular. As the government focused increas-ingly on the nationalized sector, white-collar employees in the banks and insurance and government undertakings, too, became unionized. Politicians, particularly those in the opposition, often saw the unions as an effective medium of demonstrating their strength, while unions used political support to achieve their immediate objectives. For fear of losing the support of organized labour, more often than not, the ruling party yielded to the trade unions' demands, some of which were genuine and some of which were not.

The mid-1970s witnessed the dark side of Indian democracy, with the late Prime Minister, Indira Gandhi, declaring a state of national emergency. During this period, fundamental rights, includ-ing those of trade unions, were suspended. Soon after the emer-gency was lifted in 1977, trade unionism came back with renewed vigour. It grew vertically among the officers and managers of PSUs, among university teachers, doctors and nurses in govern-ment hospitals, and lawyers. In most cases, these organizations, popularly known as guilds and associations, came up partially as a reaction to the militant unionism among the lower employees. The other factor involved was the loss of power experienced by the professionals and lower/middle-level managers, who felt that their role in decision making was dwindling. In a nationwide study of officers in the public sector, this author (Mamkoottam, 1990) found that the 'powerless' and voiceless officers organized themselves into associations to protect their interests *vis-à-vis* the workers, as well as the top management. Gradually, the (top) management, particularly in the public sector, became the weaker partner in industrial relations. The number of strikes called increased and industrial indiscipline grew, resulting in an increasing loss of mandays. Even essential services, like hospitals, the railways, airways, telecommunications and postal services, were not spared. Meanwhile, the declining productivity and poor performance of the organized sector, including that of the government, became the target of public displeasure. There was growing concern that India was lagging behind in the production of world-class products and the provision of high-quality services. It was felt that the country was thus losing out in the increasingly globalized export sector, and a large part of the blame was put on the trade unions. The trade unions, however, expressed their opposition to change time and again. They resisted initiatives for economic reform and structural adjustments, including those relating to technological change and modernization.

A key feature of industrial relations in India has been the confrontational relationship between the employer/management and trade unions, and the overwhelmingly dominant role played by the state through a plethora of labour laws. Not only are many of these labour laws archaic, but several of their provisions also considerably restrict the flexibility of labour. Flexibility is a key characteristic of modern business and industry. As discussed in the previous chapter, flexibility is an all-pervasive concept, covering the designing and manufacturing of products, production processes and labour. Labour flexibility refers to a variety of decisions relating to skills, changes in the geographical distribution of workers, occupational changes among them, and their recruitment, deployment and working hours. It is essential to consider these factors in order to maintain cost-effectiveness, productivity, quality and competitiveness in the market. The quality of flexibility has been conspicuous by its absence in the Indian labour force. Indian employers and potential foreign investors in India have been clamouring for radical changes in the existing labour legislation, to allow for greater freedom to recruit, deploy and discipline labour. It must be mentioned here that so far, no government has taken steps to initiate reforms in the country's labour legislation and in the sphere of industrial relations. In an economy such as India's, a balance in industrial relations is unlikely to be achieved unless the government initiates steps in this direction. Further, all such measures have to be supported by all the major political parties and the dominant trade unions.

Employer Strategies

Despite the rigid labour legislation and widespread protests by trade unions, many employers have undertaken modernization in recent years. They have tried to modernize the plant, restructure production processes and reorganize work. In several cases, labour has been retrenched. In the case of Associated Cement Company (ACC) versus an employees' union in a plant at Sevalia, the Gujarat High Court underlined the fact that under Section 25-FF of the Industrial Disputes Act, a company can shut down a plant or unit by transferring the title to another company.

Another interesting case is that of Hindustan Ciba–Geigy, which implemented a successful voluntary retirement scheme (VRS) for its entire 907-strong workforce at its plant at Bhandup, in the suburbs of Bombay. The success of the scheme has been attributed to its truly voluntary nature. The ability of the management to convince the union, which initially blamed it for making the plant non-viable, was of great importance in this case. The Bhandup plant, set up in the early 1960s, was the 'mother plant' of the Swiss multinational till the late 1980s, when it started making losses. The pharma division employed 1452 workers—more than three times the staff employed in the agrochem division, which employed 440. On a turnover of Rs 20 crore, the unit made a loss of Rs 7 crore. The wage bill alone was Rs 10 crore. The management threw its books open to the union, took it into confidence and offered various options. These included the possibility of selling the plant to a new owner, under whom the employees could continue to work, an employees' co-operative to operate the unit, and a VRS. The VRS provided for two options: (*a*) monthly payment of the full pension for 180 months from the date of accepting the scheme, or till 60 years of age; and (*b*) commutation of a part of the pension (not exceeding 33.33 per cent of the pension), which would be paid within four weeks of retirement, with the balance being paid monthly over 180 months, or till 60 years of age. After due evaluation of the various options, the union accepted the VRS.

Manpower has been reduced in the public sector units, too, through voluntary retirement schemes. In the Marxist-ruled state of West Bengal, known for its militant trade unionism, the workers of the Bengal Potteries *en masse* accepted a VRS. The MMTC and State Trading Corporation reduced their manpower substantially through such schemes. Some other successful cases are those of Hindustan Shipyard Limited, Delhi Transport Corporation and Bharat Gold Mine Limited. In fact, several major efforts at restructuring, by way of downsizing, are reported to have taken place among PSUs in the past few years. According to a report (*The Economic Times*, June 1, 1999), between 1993–94 and March 1999, 152 PSUs shed as many as 120,000 employees through voluntary retirement schemes. These units included sick ones as well as those which could be revived. Some of the prominent companies which laid off large numbers of employees through such schemes include the National Textile Corporation (23,000 employees), Bharat Coking Coal (9,793), HMT (4,309), and Eastern Coalfields (6,859).

However, the indiscriminate introduction of the VRS in public sector units became a cause for concern once it emerged that such schemes not only deprived the units of their best employees, but could also have disastrous consequences due to the enormous outflow of cash. Bharat Heavy Electricals Limited, which employed over 70,000 people, besides indirectly providing work to another 30,000, withdrew the VRS package offered by it once the management discovered that many of the senior and well-qualified workers and officers had availed themselves of the scheme to join the company's competitors in the private sector. Indian Drugs and Pharmaceuticals Limited, the largest pharmaceuticals company in the public sector, spent an amount of Rs 12.5 crore but lost 450 employees, the majority of whom were senior officers.

In the case of the National Textile Corporation, which has mills in many parts of the country, a revival package that rendered nearly 78,000 workmen surplus, was received enthusiastically in the initial stages. Although about 32,000 workers had opted for the scheme involving an amount of Rs 245 crore, the younger workers became suspicious of it and refused to accept it.

According to a study conducted by the All-India Management Association (AIMA) in 1993 on the human dimensions of liberalization, more organizations were able to close down parts of their business in the post-July 1991 period than earlier. The study, which covered the chief executive officers (CEOs) of 71 organizations in the organized sector, more than 75 per cent of the sample organizations had surplus labour. The study revealed that industry had been consciously opting to replace labour with capital, by judiciously introducing technological automation and organizational restructuring. Interestingly, 52.4 per cent of the respondents in the study reportedly met with no resistance from the trade unions and workers, and instead, received a positive response (*The Economic Times*, Dec. 12, 1993).

A similar survey found that 64 per cent of the companies covered by it were going through a process of restructuring and 26 per cent were planning to do so in the near future. Marketing, the organization's structure, the quality of the output, training of employees and finance were among the top areas earmarked for restructuring (*Business Today*, Jan. 7–21, 1994). The survey covered a sample of 148 chief executives, directors and vice-presidents from large, medium and small firms, spread across the major industrial centres of the country. Companies in India have, thus been downsizing to face the growing competitiveness of the market and economic recession.

Some have shed employees by shutting down operations first and later seeking legal help. As mentioned earlier, the process of legal closure is not easy and is often not granted by the government. To circumvent the protracted process, employers have resorted to shutting down operations or separating employees through voluntary retirement schemes. In the recent past, many companies, like National Rayon Corporation and the gas major, BOC have stopped production in one of their units and sought permission to close down. To avoid a legal battle and minimize protests by workers, many companies, such as Philips and Siemens, have offered attractive separation packages. Between 1995 and 1998,

Philips in India has cut down its original workforce of 10,000 by half, and Siemens by 20 per cent, by using the VRS. In sunset industries, such as the composite textile mills, the number of mills being closed is increasing every season. According to an estimate, by the end of March 1998, 93 of the 278 composite textile mills in the country had shut down production completely (*The Economic Times*, Jan. 20, 1999).

While rationalization of manpower often helps to improve operational efficiency and the health of the organization, the problem of unemployment is becoming hard to handle in the absence of a proportional rise in employment. The declining rate of employment, along with a growing GDP, has become a global phenomenon, and the trend is expected to continue even in the developed world. Most developed economies have been experiencing a decline in full-time employment, while the number of part-time workers has been growing. According to OECD sources, as much as 39 per cent of total employment in the Netherlands in 1996 was part-time, while the figures for Britain, France, Germany, Japan, Spain and the US were 22 per cent, 16 per cent, 16 per cent, 15 per cent, 9 per cent and 8 per cent, respectively. As for India, though a marginal growth in overall employment has been registered over the past few years, the growth rate has been negative in the organized sector. Once again, such developments do not encourage the trade unions and labour to support the reform process.

Labour and Trade Union Response

Experiences around the world show that the workers' response and the trade unions' strategies towards technological change vary according to the conditions in the labour market, the power structure within and around the trade unions, and the prevailing labour legislation. On the basis of three large-scale surveys undertaken in 1980, 1984 and 1990, of around 2000 British workplaces, Daniel and Millward (1993) observed widespread support for technical changes, including advanced technical changes, among both manual and non-manual workers. The support from their trade union representatives was even stronger. However, the same study pointed out that the reactions provoked by organizational changes were much more mixed. Organizational change was more often resisted than supported by manual workers. The reactions of office workers in this respect were fairly evenly balanced between favourable and unfavourable, but these employees, too, were much less supportive about organizational change than technical change.

According to Daniel and Millward, to the employees, new technology represented progress and advance. The benefits of the new machines were concrete and demonstrable, and promised competitive advantage. Investment in new technology made them feel more confident about the future, and seemed to improve their long-term job prospects and security. The workers were familiar with many features of the new technology and valued their benefits. Thus overall, the introduction of new technology tended to be associated with success. On the other hand, organizational change that was introduced independently of new equipment was more frequently associated with failure. It was often seen as an admission of unproductive organization in the past. The workers tended to view it with suspicion, as the benefits derived from different forms of organization were not self-evident to them. In their eyes, these were seen as a matter of organizational judgement. This was compounded by the fact that the idea of change was often not communicated effectively to the lower levels of employees in the organization before implementation.

Muneto Ozaki (1992) suggested in an ILO study that workers have had a limited influence on the process and pattern of technological change in most countries. An exception is Sweden, where they have played a direct role in the planning of technological change. According to the study, the unions and workers had little or no influence in this matter in Japan. The case of the workers in the machine tool industry in the US was similar. In Sweden, semi-autonomous work groups, which are funded by public policy, play a direct role in the introduction of technological change and in the creation of new work roles. As Willman (1986) suggested, the behaviour of trade unions in the face of technical change will depend upon changes in the political and economic climate, the incidence and impact of innovations, changes in the structure of unions and collective bargaining. Studies on technological change in the UK (Daniel, 1987), Italy (Treu, 1984), Australia (Deery, 1986) and Spain (Fina and Hawksworth, 1984; Mamkoottam and Herbolzeimer, 1991) show that in most cases, the management introduced technological changes unilaterally, in the face of resistance from the trade unions.

In fact, nowhere in the world have labour and trade unions keenly welcomed technological changes, and India is no exception. As mentioned earlier, the state has played a dominant role in Indian industrial relations, affecting almost every possible dimension of industrial relations. This has considerably restricted the flexibility of labour and slowed down the introduction of new technologies. In 1957, the 15th session of the Indian Labour Conference decided, in principle, to limit the possibilities of introducing technological change by adopting the 'Model Agreement'. This contained a clause for 'no retrenchment' on account of technological change. The employers were required to provide the workers with suitable alternative jobs in the same establishment or under the same employer. All along, the Indian government has followed a cautious path in the matter of changing the labour laws relating to the retrenchment of workers. In 1991, the government proposed an exit policy, which had to be abandoned due to strong opposition from the trade unions of the organized sector, including the officers' associations of various public sector companies. Gradually, the focus shifted to an approach of 'structural reforms with a human face', according to which changes in the labour laws would be introduced in phases.

It should, however, be appreciated that trade unions find it difficult to accept technological changes because they fear that the envisaged changes, if implemented, might have various adverse effects on the labour and employment situation. Major technological changes, with the accompanying structural and organizational changes, could affect the existing occupational structure, manpower skills, employment patterns and other related areas. Moreover, new technology has important implications for the structure and strategy of trade unions. The evolution of technological changes has shaped and reshaped the labour movement. As Gill (1987) suggests, perhaps it is in the history of the labour movement that the discontinuous nature of technological change can be seen most clearly.

Ranabir Samaddar (1995), on the basis of a case study of the newspaper industry, suggests that 'new technology is a weapon in the hands of the management' to eliminate trade unions. On the other hand, Roy (1995) concludes from her study of the banking industry that the worker may become an eager supporter of technological change. Studies by Akhilesh et al. (1989) show that the management mostly takes the workers for granted while introducing technological change. In general, the management tends to believe that resistance from the workers (and unions) can be overcome through monetary rewards like ex gratia benefits. All these studies have noted that efforts to introduce technological change in order to improve productivity and quality cannot succeed unless accompanied by efforts to create awareness about the new technologies among the workers.

In fact, it is worth noting that the workers (and unions) are not concerned about the introduction of technological change per se. What worries them more is the reorganization of the shop floor that results from such changes. This involves problems like the loss of jobs, internal redeployment, changes in work methods, and so on. Manik Kher (1997) notes that although the workers and unions have been resisting changes in the shop floor directly and technological changes indirectly, companies in the private sector have dealt with the workers successfully by incorporating counter-demands in their wage settlements. In a recent ILO study by this author (Mamkoottam, 1997) on 'Productivity-linked Wages in South Asia', it was found that though the management reserved the right to introduce technological changes, and to redeploy workers to enhance productivity, it always did so through a process of negotiation with the unions. It attempted to reach a settlement, under which wage increases were often made conditional to the changes to be introduced.

In a study of technological change in the steel, textile and engineering sectors in India, Kher (1997) observes variations, which may be explained by the nature of the production process, educational qualifications of the workers, the industrial relations environment and the overall economic development of the region. The attempts at modernization in these sectors were all intended to improve quality and reduce costs, but the manner of implementing the modernization programmes differed in the public and private sectors. The management in the public sector, with the remarkable exception of the Greenfield plant, was found to be complacent and lacking in commitment, with a lower morale. This sort of work atmosphere influenced the quality of the decisions taken, affecting their timeliness and reliability. In the private sector, on the other hand, decision making was quicker. The competitive spirit drove the management to display greater commitment and make concerted efforts (Kher, 1997).

Since the announcement of the new industrial policy in 1991, the trade unions registered their disapproval in several ways, including strikes on a few occasions. The trade unions in the banking, insurance and other public sector units rejected all offers for discussion. Moreover, they threatened to boycott and oppose the implementation of the measures announced for structural reforms and economic liberalization. In fact, continuous resistance from organized labour has considerably slowed down the process of reform that was envisaged in the financial, manufacturing and service sectors. However, as discussed earlier, the trade unions and labour would be co-operative if the management were willing and able to evolve a strategy of negotiation and dialogue. Recently, Escorts' management proposed to transfer 250 workers from the Rajdoot motorcycle factory to the group's tractor units. Although initially reluctant, the unions finally agreed to the redeployment. Similarly, when the Mumbai-based Philips Employees' Union submitted a charter of demands, negotiations were undertaken and a settlement was finalized eight months in advance of the expiry of the existing agreement. Another example is that of the militant Bata Mazdoor Union accepting a crucial productivity agreement which linked wages to productivity.

Although the unions have been coping with technological changes and shifting their focus of bargaining, the recent changes appear to be so swift and radical that they have nearly threatened the very foundation of trade unions. Major aspects of the new technology negate the very basis of traditional trade unionism. Flexibility, for example, questions the fixed norms regarding job profiles. Job demarcations and occupational identities are increasingly being blurred and gradually disappearing. Further, decentralization reduces collective strength by dispersing produc-tion/service centres. Unskilled and semi-skilled workers have formed the backbone of the traditional trade union centres, and their gradual reduction and elimination, together with the trend towards subcontracting, have threatened the future of the trade unions. More and more organizations are becoming smaller in size and flatter in structure, with fewer unskilled and semi-skilled workers. Above all, the new worker is better educated, well informed and more professional. His aspirations, needs and problems are different from those of the traditional worker.

Developments in recent years show that the unions in India have been unable to stop the process of restructuring, moderni-zation and other changes in the workplace, be it in the private sector or the public sector. In fact, it seems that organized labour is becoming weaker. While there has been a decline in the mem-bership rates of trade unions worldwide, it may be difficult to prove that such a decline has taken place in India. Although the total number of registered trade unions has continued to grow, the total membership of the unions submitting returns and their average membership has seen a noticeable decline since 1992. However, there is clear evidence to show that the unions' bar-gaining power has declined in recent years. The occurrence of strikes and the number of workers involved in strikes have come down. At the same time, the management's propensity for lock-outs may have grown a trend, which has been termed 'managerial militancy'. The national trade union centres appear to be losing their control over local/enterprise unions. In a recent study cov-ering collective agreements in the public sector, private (domes-tic) sector and multinationals in India, it was found that the unions agreed to the upgradation of technology, skills and restructuring of the organization/workplace if wages were linked with pro-ductivity (Mamkoottam, 1997).

The declining power of the unions may be attributed to a combi-nation of several interrelated factors. These include globalization of the economy (economic and structural changes), technological change, the attitudes of the state, employers and workers (towards unions), the occupational structure, and demographic shifts in worker profile. In some ways, the India of the 1990s may be compared to the US of the 1970s, when trade unionism started its downward journey there. Increasingly competitive prices placed pressure on the unionized employers to cut costs. Traditional collective bargaining contracts, which rigidify the internal labour markets, became less acceptable because they restricted the scope for flexibility in the allocation of resources. Many employers in the US and other countries started production in new low-wage (typically non-union) settings. Employers with unionized workers under them had to pay higher wages and found it hard to compete against firms which did not have to deal with unions. This led to the widespread adoption of strategies in favour of union avoidance and investment relocation. According to Wever (1994), workers had fewer reasons to join unions, and in some cases, saw reasons not to do so. Firms with unions came to be increasingly associated with the closure of plants and job insecurity. Similar trends have become visible in India too, in recent years.

Emerging Trends

For many decades, technological change, innovation in products and orientation towards the customer were not given priority by employers or the government in India. However, in the late 1980s to the early 1990s, international competition and the shrinking export market began to make a difference. Successive governments, including those political parties which opposed liberalization, have come to champion the cause of technological upgradation and economic reforms. No political party, except the Left (CPI/CPM in a limited sense), has taken a strong position against such changes. The traditional nexus between political parties and the trade unions affiliated to them appears to be growing weak. As U.M. Purohit of the Bharatiya Mazdoor Sangh (BMS) put it, 'Earlier, when people were disenchanted with the policies of the ruling party, they could teach it a lesson by voting it out of power in the next elections. Now what happens is that governments change but the same economic policies remain in force' (*Labour—2000*, On-line Conference, Sept. 22, 1999). An important factor related to this trend is the growing aversion of the public and media to militant unionism, which displayed little concern for the customer or the hapless citizen. It is perhaps ironic, but true, that the doctor on strike will condemn the militant banking union, while the banking employee will have no sympathy for the vocal university teacher.

Employers and the management have also started to evolve methods to bring the worker closer to the organization, while keeping the union away. In recent years, employers in India have shifted operations from highly unionized regions, such as Kerala and West Bengal, to less militant regions or to free-trade zones like the EPZ. The use of sophisticated technologies has not only reduced the size of the organization, but has also changed the type of worker employed. The labour force is increasingly coming to consist of multi-skilled, young, ambitious and career-minded workers, rather than uneducated, unskilled or semi-skilled worker. Today's worker is more interested in safeguarding his own interests than becoming an active unionist who fights for larger issues. Studies in both the UK and the US have shown that the young, educated worker, who is employed in smaller organizations, uses advanced technologies and earns comparatively higher wages, is less inclined towards trade unionism (Hundley, 1988; Disney, 1990; Ben-Israel and Fisher, 1994). Findings from Central and Eastern Europe (CEE) indicate a similar trend. Union membership in this region came down by 50 per cent during early capitalist transformation. According to Pollert (1999), trade unions in CEE have encountered structural, political and ideological problems. The decline of trade unionism has been attributed to worker apathy, anti-union employers and the contraction of large state enterprises. The growth of small private firms and services, along with self-employment and semi-informal micro-companies, has further contributed to de-unionization. Unionism is less prevalent among women, who are concentrated in services and in small and medium-sized enterprises, among white-collar workers, and among the younger workers.

As elsewhere in the world, companies in India, too, have gradually shifted their attention to developing innovative human resource policies. The attempt is to offer workers the kind of benefits that the traditional unions fought for, be it through welfare schemes, participatory fora or moves to empower the worker. In December

1996, the workers and management of Eicher Tractors Plant (Alwar), an ISO 9001 company, jointly decided to give up the practice of traditional bargaining and settled for an increase in wages, besides annual pay revisions on the basis of productivity and performance. The management also introduced other innovative schemes, especially schemes addressing the social welfare needs of the employees.

At least some managers seem to have changed their attitude towards the workers, and have realized that the reduction of excess manpower alone does not make for greater competitiveness. These managers appreciate the necessity of changing human resource management strategies while ushering in change. Professional managers realize that it is futile to fight a battle against labour in the domestic (economic) market while facing competition in the international market. Workers should no longer be seen as liabilities, but as key resources, which are to be carefully nurtured and constantly developed. A healthy work culture can be created through proactive human resource policies, and preventive measures can reduce conflict at the workplace. The slogan of the 1980s—'productivity through people'—has caught the attention of the manager of the 1990s. The management of human resources and policies relating to industrial relations must be integrated with the organization's larger corporate goals and mission. The management of personnel is no longer believed to consist of merely procedural and administrative matters, such as recruitment and salary administration. Similarly, the maintenance of cordial industrial relations is no longer viewed merely as a fire-fighting system. Instead, they are viewed as integral parts of a holistic strategy of human resource management, a strategy which is evolved at the highest level of the management. The thrust of the new human resources policy is to attract, retain and develop human resources on a continuous basis, so as to attain corporate excellence and maintain the organization's competitiveness. Professional skills are being employed to revamp the organization to create a new work culture. This culture lays emphasis on the values of enhancing quality, minimizing costs and satisfying the customer.

The top management today has to make focused efforts to understand the worker and his union. Increasingly, the managements are realizing the importance of providing a learning environment which encourages the employees to constantly upgrade their knowledge and skills. This involves both training and retraining. Other than equipping the workers to be equal to the new challenges, the managers are also learning to relate to the workers by trying to understand and empathize with them. Indian organizations today are certainly giving more importance to the development of skills for managing people, in order to communicate effectively with the subordinate employees and their unions. Managers are trying to adopt a more positive and professional approach to the management of the employees' grievances, and their attempt is to arrive at and implement negotiated collective settlements. The management of Larsen and Toubro, a large engineering concern, held prolonged negotiations with the union to initiate TQM (total quality management), Kaizen and Kanban. It reduced the working hours from 47 to 45 hours per week and effected an increase in wages, amounting to 50 million rupees per year. The result was a 10 per cent increase in productivity. Thus, as mentioned earlier, the employees and unions are not opposed to change *per se*; what they object to is the unilateral manner in which the changes are often introduced.

Modern management systems, such as TQM, Kaizen and Kanban, can be effective only if the employees are fully involved in the process. As Marshall (1992) has suggested, in high-performance systems, the employees have to be highly involved in what would earlier have been considered 'management' functions. Moreover, quality, productivity and flexibility are enhanced when production decisions are made as close to the point of production as possible. Even in a state like West Bengal, where labour has been traditionally militant, the left-controlled CITU welcomed 'participatory management'. According to the general secretary of the CITU's state unit, 'If the workers are involved in the technological upgradation process, their resistance to modernization will stop' (*Business Standard*, Dec. 22, 1994).

Agenda for the Unions

The trade unions are struggling to come to terms with the changing occupational structure and the new employee profile that is emerging. They will need to examine the workers' economic, psychological and social needs, and find ways to fulfil them. Today's workers are dissatisfied with the politicized and centralized structure of the national trade union centres, and are keen to develop enterprise unions. Clearly, decentralized unions and enterprise bargaining are seen as more market-friendly in most parts of the world. According to Pollert (1999), the general trend in the CEE region is towards decentralization, with about 90 per cent of the union's representatives reporting local agreements on basic pay. In a study of how the Manufacturing, Science and Finance union (MSF), the General Workers' union (GW), and the Engineering and Electrical Union (EEU) responded to industrial restructuring in south-west England, Upchurch et al. (2000) found that the unions were on the defensive. According to the authors, there was an abundance of grievances by individual members, but no collective response had developed to address the 'new politics of production'. The authors argue that in recent times, the control of the labour process has passed into the hands of the management, while at the same time, the work has become harder and employee discontent has grown. A more interesting, or disturbing, observation is that the ability of the collectives to control pay has been severely weakened, as pay has become increasingly individualized and performance-based. Many other such factors, including flexibility in the deployment of workers, are questioning the very basis of unionism.

The trade unions are in the process of examining the implications of the charges being made at the workplace. Some unions have even begun contemplating a shift in their philosophy, from a defensive strategy towards alternative approaches based on research and creative thinking.

As a result of globalization and industrial restructuring in the country, trade unions are beginning to make modifications in their approach to the structure, attitude and strategies to be adopted by them. Employees often prefer enterprise unions, which focus on localized bargaining, rather than the traditional, politicized and centrally controlled unions. With restructuring being undertaken at the level of the individual enterprise, workers no longer find it relevant that their unions should be driven by the guidelines issued by national centres, which are more often than not politically motivated. The new, younger worker and his union prefer to concentrate on specific issues and problems, which mostly relate to his own immediate work environment, including restructuring. For example, in April 1992, the union in TELCO signed an agreement, which recognized the management's right to redeploy and retrain workers in order to increase productivity, provided there was no retrenchment. In fact, there is a growing fear among the trade unions' leaders that the workers may revolt against them if they do not protect their immediate interests. This is precisely what happened with Kanoria Jute Mills near Calcutta, where the workers discarded the trade union and rallied under a new banner meant to take care of their own interests. The workers dismissed the directives of the union's high command and tried to resume work in the mills (Mamkoottam, 1994).

The workers, in general, have always been doubtful about the usefulness of strikes, but recently, they have become aware of their ability to assert their will against those leaders who do not keep their interest in mind. There are indications that the centralized trade union is losing ground to the independent enterprise union, which might be the union of the future. As mentioned earlier, there has been a substantial fall in the membership of unions affiliated to national trade union centres, and more and more unions prefer an independent status. Another interesting development has been the acceptance, at least in principle, by the leaders of all the national union centres that the multiplicity of unions has considerably reduced their bargaining power. In fact, on several occasions in the post-1991 period, all the different unions have come together on a common platform to protest against the government's steps towards economic liberalization and industrial restructuring. Some unions have even initiated serious discussions on the formation of a unified front. Despite such attempts, the fact remains that the tone of the unions has become less aggressive and their tenacity is on the wane.

In order to retain their relevance in the new context, the unions may need to shift their focus from traditional wage bargaining, which is characterized by quantitative *post facto* confrontational bargaining, to *ante facto* (proactive) bargaining. The latter would mean expanding the union's expertise into technological and organizational matters. What is required today is a new model of co-operative bargaining, based on an approach of continuous problem-solving, rather than the model of conflict. As in the case of the Scandinavian countries, a good part of the activities of the unions in several parts of the world are already concerned with the development of expertise within the union, so as to be able to understand technological developments and the implications of these developments on the employees' health, environment, skills, education and retraining.

In summary, this chapter has attempted to understand how far labour and industrial relations have affected the process of reform in India, and to what extent the latter has influenced the former. The political parties have had a long-standing relationship with the trade unions and have influenced their functioning. Moreover, the labour process was for long directly controlled by the state, particularly through legislation. This, in turn, discouraged bilateral relations between the labour and management. The nexus between labour and the political parties has most often impeded the process of reform. Despite major reforms in the economic and financial sectors, the government has still not introduced legislative reforms relating to labour and trade unions.

Even within this framework, however, the increasing pressure from the competitive market has spurred on many employers, including those in the public sector, to introduce various forms of organizational restructuring. Experience has shown that these changes were possible because the management made attempts to develop channels of communication, individually and collectively, with the employees. In the backdrop of the mutual dialogue between the management and labour, the trade unions have also undergone both structural and ideological changes. There is a growing perception among workers that disruptive strategies may threaten their survival in the increasingly competitive environment. There is a shift towards the co-operative model of industrial relations, as opposed to the confrontationist model. Centralized bargaining is gradually giving way to localized bargaining, which is characterized by the formation of enterprise unions.

References

Akhilesh, K. B. et al. (1989). Technological change: Management Initiatives and Trade Union Response, (unpublished draft), Banglore, Faculty of Management Studies, Indian Institute of Science.

Ben-Israel and Fisher, H. (1994). 'Organizational strategies in a changing environment'. In J. Niland, R. D. Lansbury and C. Verevis (eds), *The Future of Industrial Relations.* London: Sage Publications.

Bessant, J. (1993). 'Towards factory 2000: Design organizations for computer-integrated technologies'. In J. Clark (ed), *Human Resource Management and Technological Change.* London: Sage Publications.

Bessant, J. Paul Levy, P., Ley, C., Smith, S. and Tranfield, D. (1990). Management and organization for computer-integrated technologies. Brighton: Centre for Business Research, Brighton Polytechnic.

Braverman, H. (1974). *Labour and Monopoly Capital.* New York, Monthly Review Press.

Daniel, W. W. and Neil Millward (1993). 'Workplace industrial relations'. In J. Clark (ed), *Human Resource Management and Technical Change.* London: Sage Publications.

Daniel, W. W. (1987). *Workplace, Industrial Relations and Technological Change.* Frances Pinter, U. K.

Deery, S. (1986). 'New technology, union rights and management prerogatives: The Australian experience', *Labour and Society,* Vol. 1, no. 2. pp. 67–81.

Disney, R. (1990). 'Explanations of the decline in trade union density in Britain'. *British Journal of Industrial Relations,* Vol. 28, pp. 165–177.

Dunlop, J. (1958). *The Industrial Relations System.* London: Holt.

Ettlie, J. (1988). *Taking Charge of Manufacturing.* San Francisco: Jossey–Bass.

Fleck, J. (1987). Innofusion or diffusation? Working paper, University of Edinburgh, Department of Business Studies.

Gill, C. (1987). 'New technology and industrial relations'. In B. Turner (ed). *Industrial Relations Practice,* London: Kegan Paul Ltd.

Hundley, G. (1988). 'Education and union membership'. *British Journal of Industrial Relations,* Vol. 26. pp. 195–200.

Iyengar, J. (2000). 'A decade of reforms sees $28 billion foreign investment inflow'. *The Economic Times,* May 1.

Kher, Manik (1997). *Coping with Technological Change.* New Delhi: Response Books.

Lawler, J.J. (1986). 'Union growth and decline: The impact of employer and union tactics'. *Journal of Occupational Psychology,* Vol. 59, pp. 217–230.

Mamkoottam, K. (1990). *Managerial Unionism in India.* New Delhi: ICSSR.

Mamkoottam, K. (1994). 'Globalization and the emerging labour–management relations'. In C.S. Venkata Ratnam et al. (eds), *Labour and Unions in a Period of Transition.* New Delhi: Friedrich Ebert Stiftung.

Mamkoottam, K. (1997). *Productivity-Linked Wages in India and South Asia,* (unpublished monograph) ILO.

Mamkoottam, K. and **Herbolzeimer, E.** (1990). Interface of new technology and human resource management: A case of automobiles and textiles in Spain. (unpublished monograph) *EFMD,* Brussels.

Mamkoottam, K. and **Herbolzeimer, E.** (1991). 'Human resource implications of new technology: A case study of automobiles in Spain'. *Indian Journal of Industrial Relations,* 26 (3): pp. 205–226.

Marshall, R. (1992). 'The future role of government in industrial relations'. In M.F. Bognanno, M.M. Kleiner (eds), *Labour Market Institutions and the Future Role of Unions.* Massachusetts: Blackwell.

Pollert, A. (1999). 'Trade unionism in transition in central and eastern Europe'. *European Journal of Industrial Relations,* 5 (2): pp. 209–234.

Porter, M. (1990). *Competitive Advantage of Nations.* New York: Free Press.

Roy, Mamata (1995). 'Indian Banks, Information Technology and Bargaining'. In *New Technology and the Workers' Response* (ed) Bagchi A.K., New Delhi: Sage Publications.

Rush, H. and **Bessant, J.** (1989). Revolution in three-quarters time: Lessons from the diffusion of advanced manufacturing technologies. Brighton: Centre for Business Research, Brighton Polytechnic.

Samaddar, Ranabir (1995). 'New technology at the shopfloor level: The story of de unionisation in some Indian newspapers'. In *New Technology and the Workers Response* (ed) Bagchi, A.K., New Delhi: Sage Publications.

Treu, T. (1984). 'The impact of technologies on employment, working conditions and industrial relations'. *Labour and Society,* Vol. 1, no. 2.

Upchurch, M., Danford, A. and **Richardson, M.** (2000). Trade union response to industrial restructuring: Sectoral case studies from the southwest of England. Paper presented at the Fourth International Progressive Policy Congress, Hamburg, March 2–5.

Wever, K. S. (1994). 'On the future of trade unionism in the United States'. In J. Niland, R.D. Lansbury and C. Verevis (Eds), *The Future of Industrial Relations.* London: Sage Publications.

Willman, P. (1986). *Technological Change, Collective Bargaining and Industrial Efficiency.* Oxford: Clarendon Press.

Womack, J.P., Jones, D.T. and **Roos, D.** (1990). *The Machine that Changed the World.* New York: Maxwell Macmillan International.

Woodward, J. (1965). *Industrial Organization: Theory and Practice.* Oxford: Oxford University Press.

World Bank. (1995). *The World Development Report, 1995.* New York: The World Bank.

4

Managing Culture and Change

Introduction

As we discussed in the previous chapters, globalization and technological changes have had a major impact on the organization and its mode of functioning. In fact, the latter part of the 20th century has often been projected as an age of discontinuous change. Knowledge and information are likely to grow at a speed faster than ever before, shaping and reshaping the world and worldviews. In this context, the organization must be able to adapt itself if it is to survive, and technology and the consumer will continue to be the major stimulants for organizational change in the coming decades. The consumer is increasingly becoming global in his thinking, and is no longer confined to territorial or national boundaries. The employees of an organization, on their part, have to change their attitudes and behaviour in response to the changing environment. According to Lewin (1951), organizations should follow three steps in order to effect change successfully. These are (*a*) unfreezing the status quo, (*b*) moving to a new state, and (*c*) refreezing the new change to make it permanent. The movement from the status quo to a new state is often not easy. Unfreezing the status quo may be possible with the help of the driving forces in the given period, as these may facilitate the movement while limiting the influence of the forces restraining such a movement.

As mentioned earlier, one of the major routes to successful organizational change is by achieving a cultural transformation at all levels of the organization. The organization needs to create an atmosphere that stimulates innovation and encourages learning. According to Gresov (1984), organizations that are characterized as loosely structured, 'organic', decentralized, and/or heterogeneous tend to be more sensitive to the possibility of innovation and generate more innovations. On the other hand, organizations that are 'mechanistic', tightly structured, centralized, highly formalized, not highly differentiated and homogeneous are slower to generate innovations and less sensitive to their existence. Scholars and practitioners alike recognize that one of the most difficult barriers to organizational change is the prevailing culture and mindset of the employees/members of the enterprise/organization. Organizational culture refers to a system of shared meaning among the members of an organization, a system that distinguishes it from other organizations (Becker, 1982; Schein, 1985). This system consists of a set of key characteristics, such as values, beliefs, principles and priorities, which the organization upholds and its members are expected to adopt and practice. Every organization has a dominant culture, which expresses the core values shared by a majority of its members. It is this dominant culture which makes interpersonal and inter-group communication effective in organizations. An organization's culture can, thus, be seen as the cementing force binding its members.

Despite all the reforms initiated since 1991, India's government (political parties and bureaucracy), corporate sector (managers and workers) and trade unions are still struggling with the changing realities of the new paradigm. Many organizations have already perished in this threatening environment, while many others are trying to combat it. A combination of fear (of facing the competition) and an unwillingness to give up a protected (known) environment are perpetuating the inefficiency of several organizations. Such organizations are characterized by rigid organizational hierarchies, occupational segregation, functional isolation, one-way (downward) communication and, above all, a mechanistic culture. Many Indian organizations have failed to evolve a system of shared goals and values, and do not seem ready to face the challenges of change. Several factors are responsible for this inertia.

This chapter attempts to illustrate how the conflicts and contradictions innate in an organization's processes, together with its practices regarding human resource management, can limit its ability to change. We shall proceed to discuss the cases of two important organizations, whose operations have national and international implications. The first is the case of the National Airport Authority of India (NAA), while the second is based on a study conducted by a group appointed by the fifth pay commission at the Department of Post, Government of India (GOI), in 1995–96.

Case 1: National Airport Authority

The National Airport Authority as a corporate body was carved out of the Director General of Civil Aviation (DGCA) on June 1, 1986 by an act of Parliament. It was meant to plan and develop airports, air navigation services, ground aids, safety devices and any other related facilities. In addition to managing the domestic airports, the NAA was also entrusted with the all-important function of providing air traffic services, which include air traffic control (ATC), and the maintenance and operation of navigational aids and communication equipment for landing, taking off and overflying aircraft in and across Indian air space. In the seventh year of its operation, i.e., in 1992, the NAA re-dedicated itself to achieving the mission of 'serving the aviation industry with utmost efficiency and making flying pleasurable and comfortable in every way'. Apart from the tasks of modernizing the Delhi and Bombay airports, the NAA took it upon itself to develop 12 airports as model airports, which would be located in various parts of the country. However, as we shall see, the management has not been very successful in changing the NAA into a modern, competitive and customer-friendly institution.

Departmental Segregation

Right from the early days, the activities of ATC, and the maintenance and operation of navigational aids and communication equipment remained independent of each other. Air traffic control activities came under the directorate of aerodromes, and the latter functions under the directorate of communication, which was of communication, further divided the technical and operations branches. However, the day-to-day administration at the aerodromes and civil enclaves, including public relations, estate, housing, transport and the provision of other services at the aerodromes and civil enclaves, was the responsibility of the directorate of aerodromes and was carried out by the ATC officers. The recruitment of employees to the aerodrome and communication (both technical and operations) wings was done separately. The promotion and career prospects of the personnel were confined to their respective disciplines. As the activities and personnel of the two wings were managed by separate organizational structures, multiple lines of command existed, not only at the corporate headquarters, but also at the level of regions and field stations. As more and more advanced navigational aids and communication equipment were introduced, new posts were created in the communications wing. Over the years, this wing grew larger in size than the other disciplines. The growth in the numerical strength of officers belonging to different disciplinary groups also led to greater articulation of the problems pertaining to each group (ATC, Communication and Engineering) within the DGCA. Since the administrative units at the field stations and regional offices were placed separately and functioned independently under the two different wings, the result was duplication of manpower resources. Such duplication was required even for establishment work, administration of personnel, and disposal and despatch of correspondence. Separate bank accounts had to be maintained. The employees had to report strictly to their own disciplinary group, and the line of command was divided likewise. There was no proper clarity of roles and little appreciation of other roles.

In order to eliminate these and other structural problems, the NAA introduced a major administrative reform called 'single point administration', in 1989. It was proposed to merge the administrative units of the aerodrome and communications wings. It was also planned that a separate authority would be appointed to administer and coordinate all the different functions. These reforms, intended to achieve greater integration of and coordination among the different disciplinary groups and their operations, were to be carried out in three phases. Such reorganization was meant to eliminate the duplication of administrative machinery, and to create a focal point of accountability at the aerodromes, civil enclaves and regional level.

As a first step in this direction, the NAA created the position of Regional Executive Director (RED), who would serve as the chief of the region in areas with major regional airports. Directors from the aerodrome and communications wings were eligible to apply for the post of RED. The airport director was to be the head of the airport. He was placed above the controller of aerodromes and the controller of communications, who were redesignated as deputy directors. Officers who were of the rank of deputy directors, and who had worked in the aerodrome or communications wing for at least three years, were eligible to apply for the post of airport director. The seniormost officers from the aerodrome and communications disciplines were appointed as airport-in-charges at the various aerodromes and civil enclaves.

Once this phase of administrative reform was completed, officers belonging to the communications discipline occupied a large-number of the newly created posts. The officers of the aerodrome discipline, who had held the administrative positions at the airports till the re-organization, felt that the top management had not treated their wing fairly. In fact, they demanded the immediate withdrawal of the 'single point administration' scheme, and a reversion to the old organizational structure and administrative system. However, the officers of the communications discipline insisted on the continuation of the new system. They wanted the REDs and airport directors to be appointed strictly on the basis of merit and capability.

The ATC guild, the union of air traffic controllers, protested by calling a strike in May 1992. This resulted in serious disruption of air traffic in the country. The management then gave an assurance that the administration of the medium and small airports/civil enclaves would be carried out according to the old system. It also agreed to refer the issue of whether single point administrations should be implemented—to an external body of experts. While the body examined the issue and made recommendations, the implementation of the new scheme was to be withheld. On the strength of these assurances, the strike was withdrawn.

Officers from different disciplines, levels, regions and field stations, expressed various apprehensions regarding the new scheme.

They were of the view that single point administration had affected not only their career, but also the organizational efficiency of the NAA. We shall deal with the concerns of the officers under four headings: (*a*) perceived imbalances, (*b*) feelings of threat and deprivation, (*c*) sense of inclusion and exclusion, and (*d*) anomalies and drawbacks.

Perceived Imbalances

The officers felt that the implementation of single point administration had resulted in various kinds of imbalances in the NAA. The ATC officers, in particular, were of the view that there were serious discrepancies among their wing and the communication wing in the areas of seniority and career progression, accountability, training and experience. They argued that their career prospects were limited in comparison to those of the communication officers, and that fewer positions at the senior level were available to them. They also argued that the ATC officers had taken much longer to reach the level of ED than had the communications officers, while the latter received quicker promotions.

On taking a closer look, the discrepancies in seniority and career progression may be attributed to the fact that before the introduction of the new scheme, the recruitment and promotional policies followed in each case (aerodrome discipline and communications discipline) had been different. For example, direct recruitment at the Class-I (Group-A) level started among the officers of the communications wing in 1971, whereas for the aerodrome officers, it continued to be at the Class-II (Group-B) level till 1985. This long gap in upgrading the entry level in the aerodrome discipline must have obviously delayed the progress of the ATC officers' career. Moreover, with the introduction of new equipment, new positions had meanwhile been created at senior levels in the communications discipline.

Officers from both disciplines perceived that responsibility and accountability were not equally distributed across the two disciplines. In the eventuality of a mishap, the ATC officer on duty was held accountable, and immediate action (suspension) was taken against him. No such action was taken against the officers manning or maintaining the communications equipment. It may be mentioned here that ATC officers take decisions on the basis of the data and information provided to them by the officers and equipment of the communications department. The communications officers, on their part, were unhappy about the public visibility of the aerodrome officers, whose offices were located in such a way as to bring them in direct contact with the public. Nor were they pleased with the importance given to the aerodrome officers by way of the nomenclature attached to their designations, the differential ratings and associated allowances, and so on. Moreover, the communication officers argued that they were not adequately remunerated for their higher educational qualifications (B. Tech, M. Tech etc.). Given these feelings of mutual rejection, the officers of the two departments would naturally find it difficult to collaborate with each other to achieve the NAA's goals.

Feelings of Threat and Deprivation

The officers of the aerodrome discipline believed that their functions constituted the core activity of the NAA. They felt that all other activities were supportive in nature, and that they should be acknowledged as such. The ATC officers argued that they performed highly stressful jobs and that people beyond the age of 40–45 years could not perform such stressful activities effectively. These officers also suffered from a sense of inadequacy because they thought that their experience had little relevance in the labour market outside. They wanted appropriate steps to be taken to reroute their career within the NAA itself. In fact, they felt threatened by the introduction of single point administration, as the administrative powers and responsibilities (positions), which had till then belonged exclusively to them, had to be suddenly shared with the officers of the communications wing.

It is to be noted that at the same time, officers belonging to other disciplines, such as engineering and electronics, also experienced a severe sense of deprivation. Such feelings were aggravated by the fact that they did not have access to resources and facilities which had earlier been controlled by the aerodrome officers, and were now shared by the latter and the officers of the communication discipline. All these perceptions and discrepancies gave rise to what may best be described as feelings of inclusion and exclusion among the officers, depending on their discipline.

Sense of Inclusion and Exclusion

As discussed above, the officers of the aerodrome and communications disciplines felt threatened and deprived by each other. Even the officers of the engineering and electronic disciplines started feeling alienated. They did not feel that they were an integral part of the NAA. The engineers, for example, faced conflicting demands from the aerodrome and communications disciplines, and often found it difficult to satisfy either of them. Moreover, neither the ATC officers nor the communication officers gave them sufficient recognition or appreciation. In fact, the engineers saw no reason why they should not be considered for recruitment to the various positions in the airport management as, according to single point administration, the incumbents to these positions were supposed to be recruited on the basis of merit. Perhaps a more serious concern expressed by officers from all disciplines was that the top management had not shared information with them, particularly with reference to the proposed changes in the NAA. This naturally gave rise to feelings of exclusion.

Anomalies and Drawbacks

On closer examination, the scheme of single point administration suffered from serious drawbacks. At the regional and local levels, administrative and financial powers were centralized in the office of the RED/RCD (Regional Communications Director) and the airport director. Officers, including those who were in charge of different disciplines under the RED/RCD and airport director, often did not have sufficient decision-making powers. Inadequate delegation of power was among the major factors that could seriously weaken the middle and lower levels of the organization. Earlier, the directors/deputy directors of the different disciplines were vested with their own administrative and financial powers. In addition, the deployment of manpower was also centralized under the new scheme. This obviously led many officers across the disciplines to complain that they did not have adequate manpower to carry out their various responsibilities. It is ironical that such a situation should arise in an organization that was actually over-manned.

The NAA had accorded utmost importance to organizational restructuring and administrative reforms in order to enhance efficiency and cater to the customer. However, since the perceptions of the employees at different levels and in charge of different functions varied, the management did not receive the desired support for the reforms. The employees did not share a common goal. Nor did they realize/accept the need for mutuality and interdependence.

The lack of clarity regarding work roles, besides the lack of appreciation of others' roles and the need for interdependence, had an adverse effect on the performance of the organization. Officers often perceived of their job as being limited to the boundaries of their own discipline, instead of viewing it as an integral part of the larger corporate mission. Their approach often lacked the element of professionalism. Further, they lacked social skills and skills relating to human resources/people management. More effective channels of communication and an efficient machinery for the management of grievances could have helped manage inter-group conflicts. The polarization of officers of different disciplines could have been avoided similarly. The noteworthy feature of the case of the NAA is that the process of reform became instrumental in alienating the executives of different disciplines from the top management. The reforms further widened the chasm between these executives, instead of bringing them closer as members of an integrated team. This case illustrates that no change is likely to succeed unless the major sets of stakeholders, such as the middle-level officers, accept the need for such a change. Further, they must be encouraged to play an active role in translating this need into ideas and appropriate action.

Case 2: Department of Posts

India's Department of Posts (DOP) comprises the largest network of post offices in the world. It provides a wide range of services, including across-the-counter postal services, banking and money transfer facilities, door-to-door delivery of letters and parcels, besides many other new services. The scope and magnitude of the services offered by this vast network have played, and still play, a crucial role in the socio-economic development of the country. The DOP plays a vital role in facilitating social communication and business transactions between millions of people in India. As on March 31, 2001, there were about 154,551 post offices spread across the country. About 90 per cent of these were in rural India and the remaining 10 per cent in urban India. The DOP has a well-established structure, consisting of Postal Circle, Postal Regions, Postal Divisions, RMS Divisions, Postal Store Depots, Circle Stamp Depots and Postal Training Centres.

The new economic/industrial policy announced in 1991 had its impact on the DOP as well. As a state-controlled organization, the DOP had been functioning within the confines of bureaucratic rules, procedures and guidelines, which invariably make for a rigid, and ultimately obsolete, service organization. In the post-1991 scenario, the DOP began to feel the pressure to shift from its bureaucratic culture to a decentralized, deregulated, market-friendly and customer-oriented system. In order to survive in a market-driven economy, it had to become forward-looking and needed to develop a professional business culture. The emerging environment made it imperative for the DOP to go beyond philanthropy and provide value-added services to the customer; and for this, the organization needed to undergo a complete metamorphosis. The customers, who were now in a position to choose from a variety of alternatives, expected prompt, polite, cost-efficient and high-quality service.

With the spread of the IT revolution, electronic systems of information transfer were developing very rapidly. In many parts of the world, post offices were being connected to online networks to create information centres. Their operations were increasingly being influenced by the use of electronic mail, mail order, and digital network. Further, they were distributing information on everyday life through facsimile video decks, telex and data terminals. Major technological innovations had transformed postal services in many countries. Bulk high-breed 'electronic-based' type of services were being offered in Sweden, the UK, Canada and Australia. Given these developments, the DOP had no choice but to modernize itself and take full advantage of the technological innovations.

Several committees and study teams appointed in the past had suggested selected policy interventions. Among the important items on the agenda for change were the modernization of services, introduction of appropriate technology, rationalization and re-organization of the management structure, and rationalization of the policy relating to personnel. The DOP initiated several steps in an attempt to redefine its role in society. Its new mission was to set up a model, customer-driven and efficient postal service.

In order to achieve this mission, it developed a three-pronged strategy of (*a*) modernization/induction of advanced technology; (*b*) inculcation of a spirit of competitiveness through creativity and innovation; and (*c*) reorientation of its approach to human resource development, as well as structural reorganization.

The DOP launched a series of modernization programmes. These attempted to introduce innovative and value-added services, such as hybrid mail service, satellite money order, corporate money order, automatic mail process, speed post service, metro channel, *rajdhani* channel, express parcel service and business channel. The DOP also drew up a plan for restructuring the organization with the aim of establishing a flat structure. Among the top priorities were administrative decentralization, with particular emphasis on the devolution of financial power, and the establishment of a technology-driven system characterized by functional accountability and responsiveness to the customer's requirements.

Business Restructuring and Human Resources

As emphasized already, technological innovations and the introduction of modern equipment must go hand in hand with new ways of managing human resources. Even the most attractive products/services and sophisticated technologies can become nonproductive unless the employees are equipped and ready to deal with them. In this sense, technological change and modernization go beyond the machine, and include the human skills and attitudes which make them workable.

Human Resource Profile

The DOP has been a labour-intensive organization, and at the time of the study (1995–96), it was manned by 598,000 personnel. It consisted largely of non gazetted officers. It had 1,326 gazetted officers, 17,209 supervisory staff, and a total of 587,588 clerical/other staff. Barring the few officers, who were recruited directly through the Indian Postal Service Examination (IPS), more than 90 per cent of the employees entered the organization at the nongazetted level, 69 per cent of them as Group C employees. These employees belonged to different regions. They had different profiles, in terms of age, length of service, educational qualifications, the level at which they entered the organization and the current level in the organization. A sample survey showed that nearly 75 per cent of the employees of the department were above 40 years of age, and more than 38 per cent above the age of 51 years. About 54 per cent of the Group 'A' officers and 100 per cent of the Group 'B' officers were above the age of 40 years. Eighty-six per cent of the employees had more than 10 years of work experience, 67 per cent more than 20 years, and 52 per cent more than 25 years.

Organizations with employees of higher age and longer durations of service are likely to be less agile and less willing to accept change. However, in the case of the DOP, this negative feature was offset, to a large extent, by the comparatively better educational profile of the employees. More than 50 per cent of them were graduates or had educational qualifications of an even higher level.

Employees' Perceptions

Employees at all levels in the DOP displayed a certain degree of introspection when they admitted that the image and efficiency of the organization had deteriorated over the years. The anxiety to change to meet the challenges of the emerging environment was also widely shared among the employees. They were conscious of the fact that the modern customer had a different profile, and demanded services of better quality and speed. Interestingly, most employees did not feel that the customers' demands were unjustified, although the older employees, with longer years of service, were a bit reluctant to accept the new reality. The employees were aware of the competitive services provided by the private agencies, which were more customer-friendly and better managed, although more costly. Once again, the older employees appeared reluctant to acknowledge the competitive environment and the emerging threat posed by the private courier/agency services.

Barring a few of the older people with longer years of service, the employees had a positive attitude to the possibility of improving the efficiency of their services. They were not only conscious of the need to enhance the quality of the services provided to the customer, but were also optimistic about managing it.

Employees' Response to Modernization

With the march of modernization, steps were taken to improve the physical appearance, hygiene and infrastructure of the workplace. These changes were welcomed by the employees, who saw no reason to be unhappy about improvements in their working conditions. The environment and hygienic conditions of the workplace had been far from desirable in most post offices. Some of the workplaces lacked sufficient lighting and ventilation. They were not furnished properly and lacked the requisite equipment. Some offices were exposed directly to the scorching heat of the summer and the cold of the winter.

At the individual level, the employees were not against computerization and modernization *per se*. In most cases, those who were working on the computerized, multi-purpose counter machines were quite happy about the change. They said that their work had become less strenuous and more efficient, compared to the days when they were performing the same operations manually. However, they felt that they were not given sufficient training in computer operations and the use of the relevant software. Wherever the management had made a conscious effort to provide training, the employees enjoyed the new mode of working. Further, there was substantial improvement in their efficiency and productivity.

Areas of Concern

At the time of the study, while the DOP had reason to be proud of its vast network and experienced manpower, there were also reasons for concern. The employees appeared to have lost pride in their organization and the job they were doing. There was a widespread feeling among them that their organization was being neglected by the government. They were dissatisfied with the financial allocations, granted to the DOP and the lack of autonomy in decision making. In addition, they were not pleased with the infra-structural facilities, salaries and perks. Such feelings, of course, could not support a healthy organizational culture. While a small percentage of the employees (at all levels) were dedicated and highly motivated, the large majority appeared to be demotivated. They had a low level of self-esteem and felt a sense of alienation from the organization.

Officers and employees across different levels and regions complained about the existing promotional avenues, salaries and other forms of reward, and their lack of relation to merit and/or performance. They did not feel free to take individual initiatives and were unhappy that they were not encouraged to use their creativity at work. As the DOP is so highly dependent on human resources, it can ill afford to neglect the potential contributions of its employees. Further, both the employees and trade unions felt very strongly that the DOP should be given more autonomy and powers to decide its policies on its course of action. Nor were they satisfied with the way the management dealt with their grievances. It may be mentioned here that if the employees find their organization's attitude to them inequitable and unfair, they are likely to lack motivation and commitment to the organization.

In a survey conducted in 1989, the employees had expressed the view that the management did not appreciate good work and did not give them adequate promotional opportunities. They lacked the autonomy to implement new ideas and the organization did not encourage them to participate in decision making. The survey also found that the level of satisfaction fell with the level of the employee and his/her level of education. Another finding was that a good many officers had very low levels of motivation, self-esteem and initiative. They lacked a sense of direction, purpose and social worth. However, most customers found the postal employees honest, hard-working and courteous.

However, the consumers included in the study of 1995–96, do not share the same views. Many employees, particularly those dealing with the customers, are largely perceived to be discourteous. This change in perception could either be a result of the heightened expectations of the customer, or the deterioration in the attitude of the employees, or a combination of both. As we have seen, the management of human resources left much to be desired and was not linked to the organization's objectives. The DOP failed to professionalize the management of human resources.

Among the issues raised most frequently by the employees was that they were not clear as to whether the DOP was expected to operate as a pure service organization which provides essential services, or as a commercial organization operating on business principles. This question was often raised by executive and non-executive employees alike, and the confusion in this sphere compounded the feelings of frustration and helplessness.

Some other contentious issues were the expansion of the network, the launching/diversification of products and services, as well as their pricing. Employees from different levels of the hierarchy, age-groups and experience expressed concern about the indiscriminate opening of branch offices in areas where such operations could not be justified. An overwhelming majority of the employees was in favour of differential pricing of products, instead of the blanket policy of subsidized pricing. In brief, the employees were either not aware of the objectives of their organization, or did not find them viable and meaningful. The organization could have better harnessed the potential of its employees if it had taken appropriate steps to clarify its objectives and mission to the employees.

Modernization and its Implications for Manpower

New technology invariably replaces manpower, substantially in some cases and marginally in others. Many of the modern process and production technologies are meant to reduce human intervention so as to improve productivity and quality, be it in the manufacturing sector or service sector. In the DOP, excess manpower posed a major problem in terms of cost. In an effort to reduce the increasing gap between its revenue and expenditure, the DOP had imposed a total ban on the creation/expansion of posts in 1983. It is reported that during the 1990s, the volume of work handled by the organization grew by nearly 9 per cent, while there was a reduction of 5–6 per cent in operative manpower. Together with the ban, a decision was taken to redeploy the redundant manpower. (The government decided to discontinue sorting of mail in the running trains.)

The major operations of the organization were based on certain norms known as the 'Marathe Time Test', developed in 1951. Although over the years, there were changes in the volume of traffic, various work procedures, technology, the working conditions and the employees' profile, the outmoded norms were not changed. Strangely, shortage of manpower was often cited as a major reason for the declining efficiency of the organization. On a cursory examination of the activities in various workplaces and detailed discussions with the officers, wide variations were found to exist in the manning patterns in different areas of activity and different regions. These ranged from an obvious surplus of manpower to an acute shortage of manpower.

Supervision and Promotional Policies

As we have seen, the work norms followed in the organization were outdated. Further, their implementation and monitoring was poor, if not nonexistent. The supervisors who were expected to closely monitor the operations of the subordinate staff, were seldom seen to be performing this duty. This could be partially explained by the absence of reasonable norms and effective monitoring mechanisms. A more important reason could be the supervisors' lack of supervisory skills and the feelings of demotivation arising from this. The supervisory officials in the administrative cadre appeared to have many serious complaints, particularly those relating to promotions.

The supervisory positions in the administrative and operative cadres were filled by officers promoted from the lower cadres. While the supervisory positions were filled through a process of time-bound promotion, the positions at the middle level (i.e., the Group 'B' officers) were filled through departmental examinations. This sort of promotion policy resulted in the creation of a supervisory cadre which very often lacked the basic supervisory skills. Thus, the supervisors were below par in the areas of inter-personal relations, communication and negotiation. The lower-level, non-executive employees were given two time-bound promotions, without ensuring that they possessed the minimum educational qualifications and the necessary supervisory skills. Many employees reached the supervisory positions only at an older age. By this time, most of them had lost their enthusiasm to exercise their initiative and leadership skills, both of which are essential determinants of the performance of a supervisor.

To make matters worse, the pay scales of the supervisory staff and the employees in the operative cadres were anomalous. While the former was on the scale of Rs 1400–2300, the operative cadre (of HSG-2) was on a scale of Rs 1600–2660. The supervisors argued that despite this, they were expected to take on various responsibilities of a managerial and executive nature, including inspections, technical management checks and controlling the subordinate staff. They also had statutory powers to exercise disciplinary authority over the operating staff, including those at the HSG-2 level. Naturally, with the supervisors being in the same grade, or even worse, in a lower grade than the operating staff, the execution of supervisory functions suffered. Moreover, the anomalies resulted in an erosion of the supervisors' authority. It is no surprise, then, that there was a great deal of frustration among the employees of this cadre.

Performance-based Wage and Reward Systems

Victor Vroom (1964) developed one of the most comprehensive theories of motivation. He suggested that the tendency to act in a certain way depended on the strength of the expectation that a given outcome would follow the act, as well as on the attractiveness of that outcome to the individual. Vroom's theory highlights the crucial linkage of performance with reward on the one hand, and with effort, on the other. The major force behind the performance of an individual is his belief that performing at a given level will bring him the desired outcome and his perception that expending a given amount of effort will result in a level of performance that is sufficient to achieve the desired outcome.

Vroom's theory clearly suggests that in order to get the best out of the employee, there is need to (a) measure performance and monitor effort, and (b) relate compensation to the effort expended by the employee. This is obviously based on the assumption that an employee will put in only that amount of effort which he perceives is necessary to achieve the outcome (reward). Such a perception could, in principle, lower the level of performance unless better rewards are linked with higher levels of performance. In addition, a sense of equity is also important to employees at all levels. As Veechio (1984) suggests, the employee's perception of what he gets from a job (outcome) is related to what he has put into it (input); the employee then compares his input–outcome ratio with the input–outcome ratio of relevant others. These relevant others consist of colleagues within the organization and others in comparable positions outside the organization.

The practice of paying overtime (OT), for example, has always posed a major problem for the DOP. In fact, OT formed a significant proportion of the employees' income. The OT earned by a sorting assistant, for example, was estimated to amount to as much as 100 per cent of his salary. In the post globalized era, particularly after 1985, the DOP, like many other organizations, took deliberate steps to reduce/eliminate the payment of OT. OT bills had driven several enterprises to bankruptcy in many industries in India and elsewhere. In recent years, many organizations have succeeded in replacing the unproductive practice of OT with more meaningful methods, including incentive schemes, performance-based pay and productivity bonuses.

In January 1996, the DOP's operations were seriously affected when employees in Delhi and Bombay resorted to partial strikes and go-slow against the reduction/elimination of OT. However, the employees and trade unions expressed a keen interest in the idea of linking monetary compensation with the performance/effort of the employee. They also felt that the existing system did not adequately compensate those who performed well, while compensating the non-performers. Employees at all levels were of the view that the compensation package should be restructured in such a way that a part of the salary should be directly linked to performance and productivity.

Trade Unions and Industrial Relations

Harmonious industrial relations are important for the efficient functioning of an organization. Besides, industrial relations have always played a crucial role in facilitating/hindering organizational change and technological innovation. The industrial relations climate of the DOP was similar to that of most other organizations belonging to the state (public) sector. The union density was as high as 100 per cent. As in several other public-sector organizations, the officers, including senior executives, were members of officers' associations. Reflecting the national pattern of unionization, the DOP employees belonged to different unions, which, in turn, were affiliated to different national trade union centres. The multiplicity of political affiliations and the rivalry created by this among the unions reflected on the DOP's workforce. The employees were divided on the basis of their affiliation to different unions, whose policies are determined by political ideologies rather than business/organizational issues. This weakened the DOP's ability to adapt to the changing environment.

While at the individual level, the employees were enthusiastic about technological change and computerization, at a collective level, they (particularly the trade unions) had certain reservations. The unions, though not against modernization and computerization *per se*, were particularly concerned about the possible effects of computerization on the employees' workload and remuneration. They were also worried about the prospect of loss of jobs.

However, it is important to note that the employees and unions, in general, accepted the need for modernization and technological change. They also accepted the fact that the quality of services had declined, thus tarnishing the image of the organization among the customers. Another significant and positive factor was that the unions, at large, were anxious to improve the quality, reliability and speed of the DOP's services. They sought a revision of the tariff structure to make the organization's operations financially viable; they supported computerization and automation, although not unconditionally; they were for the revision of the payment system on the basis of performance; they were keen on adding new products/services and wanted better training to be provided to the employees. The unions wanted the top management to be given more financial and administrative powers, and sought further decentralization of power at the regional level.

However, the unions were against the privatization of services, which had traditionally been provided exclusively by the DOP. They were also against any reduction of manpower or an increase in the workload. They were against any reform that might reduce the number of positions at the non-executive levels, or increase the number of posts at the managerial levels. Thus, the major apprehension of the trade unions appeared to be related to the loss of jobs and reduction of manpower, which, in turn, would affect the unions' strength as well. Above all, the unions were opposed to the idea of the management taking unilateral decisions; they wanted to be consulted and associated with the management before changes were introduced.

Experience, the world over, has shown that the management has been more successful in introducing changes whenever it has consulted the trade unions and associated them with the decision-making process. The fears and resistance of the unions can often be explained by incomplete information and inadequate knowledge of the situation. Applebaum et al. (2000), who conducted a study based on research data collected from a large number of plants, concluded that companies are, indeed, more successful when the managers share their knowledge and power with the workers (subordinates), and when the subordinates assume greater responsibility and discretion. The study which covered steel, apparel, and medical electronics and imaging plants, revealed that wherever the workers formed self-directed teams, they were able to eliminate bottlenecks and coordinate the work process. When they worked as members of task forces created to improve quality, they communicated with individuals outside their own work groups and were able to solve problems.

Expensive equipment in the steel mills was operated with fewer interruptions. The costs of turnaround and labour were cut in the apparel factories. Further, the inventories of components and medical equipment became less costly. The survey of the workers showed that jobs in a participatory work system often provide the workers with more challenging tasks and more opportunities for creativity. Moreover, the workers were less likely to report that they had been made to work overtime involuntarily. Conflicts with their co-workers were also reduced, and they were more likely to be satisfied with their surroundings.

Management of Change and a Learning Organization

As mentioned earlier, postal services have undergone major changes in many parts of the world. Countries such as Australia, Britain and Canada have commercialized, for-profit post offices, which remain a government-owned monopoly. In countries like Holland and Germany, there are for-profit post offices that retain a monopoly status, but are owned by private shareholders. Even though the post offices in Australia, the UK and Canada are a government-owned monopoly, they have decidedly become more businesslike. The Canada Post Corporation (CPC) is government-owned, but enjoys considerable commercial freedom. Though not specifically for-profit, the company has interpreted its financial mandate of 'self-sufficiency' to mean a search for profitability, in order to generate adequate resources for continued investment and expansion (see NALC Postal Record, 1997).

The British Post Office has been making profits continuously for many years. Restructured in 1986, it consists of a single board of directors which runs three subsidiaries that deal with each other on a strictly commercial basis. These three are the Royal Mail, which processes and delivers letters; the Parcel Force, meant for packages; and Counters, the retail network which serves the other two subsidiaries, as well as private banks and government agencies. The managers who run the British Post Office are seeking fundamental changes in the way delivery work is organized. Armed with theories of TQM, the Royal Mail aggressively advocated 'team-working' as a way of boosting the efficiency of the business in the face of growing competition. According to this approach, letter carriers with contiguous routes would be grouped together, given collective responsibility for a geographic area and assigned a team leader (essentially a line manager). The latter would evaluate the performance of the team rather than of individuals.

Among the world's government-owned post offices, it is the Australian Postal Corporation (APC) which is perhaps the most commercially oriented. In 1989, the labour government of the day transformed the Australian Postal Commission into a for-profit corporation, which, however, remained government-owned. The resulting body retained a monopoly on letter mail delivery, in return for providing universal service. The APC is no different from any other private company in Australia, except that all its shares are owned by the national government. Its management and the union decided on a 'team-working' system, which was introduced by an agreement reached through collective bargaining in 1994. The system is still in the process of being developed. As an outgrowth of a programme similar to employee involvement, called industrial participation, the system involved teams of eight to 10 letter carriers, headed by a leader. The APC is one of Australia's most successful companies in terms of profitability and customer satisfaction.

Few countries have received more attention in the sphere of postal services than New Zealand. It was among the first to commercialize its post office (NZ Post) in the 1980s. Though still a state-owned enterprise, NZ Post has been run like a private company since 1987, with an eye on the bottom line. The company raised its prices and imposed higher delivery fees on rural residents. It slashed its employment almost by half and closed more than 500 of the nation's 1200 post offices, replacing them with private franchisees who provided minimal services. It also eliminated unprofitable offerings. This brought in surging profits and accolades from the country's business community—NZ Post was voted Company of the Year in 1994. During the late 1990s, the government approved its bid to merge with Express Freight Services, New Zealand's largest shipper of parcels.

There are other examples of state-owned enterprises transforming themselves from bureaucratically controlled, inefficient and non-responsive systems to market-driven, customer-oriented and performance-based organizations. Arnel (1997) has examined the evolution and implementation of a range of reforms at Victoria Office Building in Australia. The reforms included large-scale downsizing and organizational restructuring, achieving quality certification, the introduction of methods of measuring performance, and the implementation of commercial and competitive business practices. Arnel's case study is, in fact, an illustration of how a planned programme can fundamentally alter the culture of an organization from a bureaucratic, rigid one to a market-driven, customer-oriented one.

The two Indian organizations examined by us, namely, the NAA and the DOP, have not been quick enough to respond to the changing environment. However, the DOP has fared comparatively better than the NAA in this respect. Since the late 1990s, it has taken major initiatives to modernize the organization. The areas of reform include the process of operations and the structure of products/services. Major efforts have been made to computerize both the operational and administrative activities. Realizing that the new system of interactive communication would pose a challenge to the traditional postal products and services, the DOP has taken steps to convert the traditional post office into a logistic player with all the modern communication networks. In fact, efforts are afoot to make the local post office a full service distribution centre. Thus, in addition to being a mail centre, the post office will also become the hub of information, the local warehouse and a centre for communication. The DOP has begun collaborating with various institutions/banks that deal with mutual funds, securities, pension funds, and so on, so as to be able to dispense a large number of financial services/products. The department aims to serve as a bridge between the e-penetrated virtual world and the real world.

The reasons for the adoption of differing approaches by the NAA and the DOP could be varied and are difficult to identify in measurable terms. It can be said, however, that the very survival of the DOP was being threatened by the severe competition posed by the private courier companies, on the one hand, and newer communication channels, such as the internet and e-mail, on the other. Thus, the pressure to modernize would have been greater. However, perhaps a more important factor is the dynamic leadership of the top management. The leadership took major steps to introduce a variety of new products, which are not only innovative, but also competitive. Deliberate attempts were made to create a competitive, customer-oriented and innovative environment in the DOP. The department's efforts to develop the necessary wherewithal in terms of organizational and human resources played a significant role in helping it respond effectively to the changing demands of the environment.

Further, the top management of the DOP realized that the organization's core competency is its vast network and large manpower resources and, thus, made noteworthy attempts to retrain/re-equip the employees, taking full advantage of its core competencies.

The officer/managerial cadres of the DOP are trained at the Postal Staff College at Ghaziabad, while the non-executive staff members receive training at one of five regional training centres situated in different parts of the country. The organization, which wanted to expand not only its operational network but also the nature of the services and products offered, obviously needed to develop technical and managerial skills among the employees. For this reason, the DOP collaborated with various institutes of technology and management. The employees and trade unions appreciated the efforts to train them, and wanted the training facilities to be decentralized, so that they were more easily available at the local level. The employees and the management alike considered the training useful, as well as necessary for the improvement of the organization's performance.

The cases of the DOP and the NAA illustrate, though differently, that the introduction of structural changes has little or no impact unless major initiatives are taken to promote an appropriate organizational culture. Unlike the NAA, the DOP management took major initiatives to prepare and develop human resources, which alone can conceive of and implement change. It made serious attempts to create a learning environment, so that the employees could appreciate the changes taking place and adapt themselves effectively to the competitive market.

As Argyris (1978) suggest, one of the biggest tasks of the 21st century organization is to minimize anti-learning actions. Innovation and learning are considered to be crucial for the survival of organizations in this millennium. In his path-breaking book, *The Fifth Discipline*, Senge (1990) illustrates how a learning organization is one which has developed the capacity to adapt and change continuously. As Mayo and Lank (1994) argue, learning goes beyond the acquisition of knowledge and information; it is about acquiring information and knowledge, and also doing something differently as a result. Those who treat learning as a business process will be the ones to succeed in the increasingly competitive 21st century.

References

Applebaum, E., Bailey, T., Berg, P. and Kallenberg, A. L. (2000). *Manufacturing Advantage*. New York: Cornell University Press.

Argyris, C. and Schon, D. (1978). Organizational learning: Theory, method and practice. Reading: Addison Wesley.

Arnel, T. (1977). Changing attitudes: From bureaucracy to market forces (A case study of leadership development in the Victorian Office Building). www.psmpc.gov.au/media/session p.7

Becker, H.S. (1982). 'Culture: A sociological view'. *Yale Review*.

Business Today. (1994). 'Mega Groups: Finding the Focus', January 7–21.

Gresov C. (1984). 'Designing organizations to innovate and implement: Using two dilemmas to create a solution'. *Columbia Journal of Business*, Winter pp. 63–67.

Lewin, K. (1951). *Field Theory in Social Science*. New York: Harper and Row.

Mayo, E. and Lank, E. (1994). The power of learning: A guide to gaining competitive advantage, Institute of personnel and development, London.

NALC homepage (1997). Reshaping the postal service to fit a changing world. *Postal Record*, 110(7). http://www.nalc.org.

Schein, E.H. (1985). *Organizational Culture and Leadership*. San Francisco: Jossey–Bass.

Senge, P. (1990). *The Fifth Discipline: The Art and Practice of the Learning Organization*. New York: Doubleday.

Veechio, R.P. (1984). 'Models of Psychological Inequity'. *Organizational Behaviour and Human Performance*, October, pp. 266–282.

Vroom, V. H. (1964). *Work and Motivation*. New York: John Wiley and Sons.

5
Productivity Bargaining and Change

Introduction

The growing competitiveness of the market economy exerts constant pressure on organizations to improve their productivity and performance. The many experiments conducted by W.J. Taylor, including his studies of time and motion and of incentive schemes, had emphasized the importance of linking wages with productivity. In fact, Taylor believed monetary reward to be the only factor which could motivate employees to improve their productivity. Although subsequent research and thought have limited, if not invalidated, the application of Taylor's thesis, the importance of improving productivity remains unquestioned, as does its linkage with wages.

There was a renewed focus on efforts to link wages with productivity in the 1960s, when Flanders (1969) introduced the concept of productivity bargaining. The first productivity agreement was signed at ESSO's Fawley Refinery, near Southampton, in the UK in February 1960. This marked the beginning of a new pattern in the management of industrial relations. Extensions of this pattern can be seen in India and many other countries which practise the industrial relations system and collective bargaining. However, different countries have come up with different modifications and adaptations, depending on the conditions prevailing in the country.

The rapid economic progress of Japan and the subsequent success of the East Asian nations in recent years once again focused attention on the improvement of productivity. The globalization and liberalization of the South Asian economies brought productivity-related issues into the limelight. The concepts of productivity and wages are very complex and involve several factors, including technology, management, raw material, energy and labour input.

What is Productivity?

Productivity has been defined in different ways. Productivity, in a broad sense, means output per unit of input of productive resources, including labour/manpower. The most frequently used measure of productivity is probably output per unit of labour time expended, which, in fact, would indicate labour productivity. Higher productivity means accomplishing more with the same amount of resources; or producing the same output, at constant or improved quality, with less input. Productivity, therefore, is not only about the efficient use of labour alone, but of all resources, including technology, capital, raw materials, energy, information, management and other intangibles. In other words, productivity refers to the overall effectiveness and performance of organizations.

Productivity is affected by certain internal and external factors, whether directly or indirectly. The external factors include government policies and institutions, the socio-political and economic conditions, business climate, availability of finance, energy and raw materials, transport and communications. The internal factors can be divided into hard and soft ones, according to Shaheed (1994). The hard factors include products, technology, equipment and raw materials, while the soft factors are the people in the organization, the organization's systems and procedures, the style of management and work methods. Among these, the workers and managers play a particularly important role. The contributions made by the people of an organization vary according to their ability and willingness to contribute. While there are many factors which contribute to the extent of motivation of an employee, wages may be considered one of the more important ones. Consequently, wages would also have a significant effect on the improvement of productivity.

Pay Systems

The major objective of an efficient pay system should be to attract, retain and motivate employees to constantly improve their performance and, thereby, achieve the organization's objectives efficiently. While evolving such a pay system involves several issues, external competitiveness, internal equity, the employer's capacity to pay and the economic conditions prevailing in the state/country are important considerations. There are different types of pay systems, such as time-rate, piece-rate, measured day rate and so on. Under the time-rate system, an employee's pay is predetermined for the given quantum of time for which he has been engaged, irrespective of any variation in his performance during that period. In contrast, under payment by result (which is based on the piece-rate system), at least a part of the pay varies with measured changes in the employee's performance. The measurement of these changes is based on predetermined rules.

The system of payment by result can be based broadly on three considerations. The first is piece-work, or the units or pieces produced. The second type may consist of a bonus system, which can be based on several factors, including the units or pieces produced, the time taken for production *vis-à-vis* the time allowed, quality, the utilization of machines and materials, attendance, factors leading to savings/elimination of wastage, and so on. The third type focuses on the reduction of costs, so the major considerations are the ratio of labour costs or other defined costs to the physical measure of output, the sales value of production, and the total costs of production or value added (workers share all or a part of the difference between the actual and expected costs). Such systems may be based on individual performance, the performance of a group/team of workers, or the performance of the plant or enterprise as a whole.

Payment by result came into use in the 1920s and was quite popular by the time of the Second World War. However, the system suffered a setback in most countries during the 1960s, especially in the organized sector, perhaps due to the erosion of the standards of performance. While this period saw an improvement in the standards of living, it also saw a change in the workers' attitudes. The workers were now more concerned with the stability of their earnings, together with a congenial and safe working environment, rather than with better financial rewards in return for increased work pressure. In fact, from the 1960s, employers had begun investing more in mechanization and automation, rather than in trying to increase the productivity of labour and improving performance. The employer's attention had shifted towards better quality, and cost-effective utilization of plants, machinery, raw materials and energy.

However, since the 1980s, there has been a renewed interest (in most developed countries) in differential pay systems based on performance. The measurement of performance may encompass the performance of groups, or the entire plant or enterprise, in addition to the evaluation of individual performance. This renewed interest in differential pay systems based on performance may be partly explained by the technological changes that have taken place in the workplace. The introduction of modern technologies has also brought group work into sharper focus, while at the same time, empowering the individual employee so that his contribution to the group, as well as to the plant/enterprise as a whole, improves. Japan's successful experience in reconstructing its economy has also been partially responsible for the revival of interest in linking the pay system with productivity.

In order to be able to compete with the developed world, Japan's government, firms and people started a productivity movement in the 1960s. This movement was aimed at (*a*) linking an improvement in productivity with an increase in employment (by making efforts to prevent unemployment); (*b*) encouraging co-operation between labour and the management in the designing and implementation of measures, so as to improve productivity; and (*c*) distributing the gains resulting from improved productivity among the management, labour and consumers, subject to the conditions of the national economy (Inouye, 1994). The success of the Japanese industries in improving their levels of productivity, quality and competitiveness cannot be overstated. Their achievements were the result of the combined contributions made by labour and the management, in addition to investment in modern technology and improved utilization of capital. It must be noted that a practice common to all the Japanese companies was an attempt to link part of the wages with productivity.

The case of Singapore is another interesting one. The country went through a major recession in 1985. This highlighted the inefficiency of the rigid pay system, among other things. In 1986, a subcommittee of the National Wage Council recommended a flexible pay system, as against the existing system based on seniority. According to this system, (*a*) wages should reflect the value of the job; (*b*) wage increases should lag behind growth in productivity; (*c*) a company's profitability and the performance of the individual should be taken into account while increasing wages; (*d*) wage increases on the basis of the performance of a company or an individual should not always be a permanent feature; and (*e*) there should be a measure of stability in the worker's income. This system was implemented in both the public and private-sector enterprises in Singapore. Some of the interesting features of the new wage system are briefly discussed below:

1. The wage structure was composed of the basic wage, an annual wage supplement (AWS) of one month's basic wage, and a variable wage component of about two months' basic wage.

2. Wages should reflect the value of a particular job, hence the range in salaries should not be too wide. Ideally, a ratio of 1:5 was to be maintained between the maximum and minimum.

3. The service increment built into the basic salary was to be small (2 per cent) under normal circumstances. It would be given in recognition of a worker's length of service, loyalty and experience.

4. The variable component, which would be based on the company's performance, was to be paid annually or semi-annually.

Wage Determination in India

The government of (independent) India in 1947 initiated a series of legislative and other measures to improve the conditions of employment and industrial relations. The Industrial Disputes Act, 1947, played a significant role in the area of wage fixation in the country. The evolution of a wage policy may be traced back to the Industrial Truce Resolution of 1947. Subsequently, a number of committees, commissions, wage boards and tribunals were set up to determine the wages of workers at different levels in the government, as well as the public-sector and private-sector enterprises. The passage of the Minimum Wages Act, 1948, the appointment of the Fair Wages Committee (also in 1948), and the setting up of various tribunals to settle the wage demands of workers in several industries illustrated the government's intention to regulate the process of setting wages. Several government-appointed committees, such as the S. Chakraborty committee and the Arjun Sengupta committee, deliberated upon the parameters for determining the wages of industrial workers in India, and recommended different steps in this regard. These committees, among other things, reiterated that industrial workers were governed by the Industrial Disputes Act of 1947, and that their remuneration levels and patterns should be determined through collective bargaining (except in cases where special wage boards were set up for the same purpose).

As we have already discussed, different kinds of changes have been introduced in the Indian corporate sector, including productivity-linked wages, in the aftermath of the reforms introduced in 1991. This chapter is based on data collected as part of an ILO–SAAT study on 'Productivity-linked Wages in India and South Asia'. The study covered a number of collective agreements between the management and unions in the public sector, private sector and the multinational corporations operating in India. These were analyzed to understand the processes by which settlements were reached on productivity-linked wage systems, and the contents and outcomes of such agreements. A structured questionnaire was distributed to the management of the enterprises covered, with the aim of assessing the impact of such agreements on productivity, the wage earnings of workers, overtime, absenteeism, the cost of labour, the deployment of manpower and industrial relations. The study found considerable variations in the backgrounds within which the productivity-linked wage agreements were made. The contents and outcomes of such agreements also varied, depending on the organization and whether it belonged to the private (domestic) sector, public sector, or a multinational corporation.

Process of Wage Determination

As a practice, the management of a public sector enterprise (PSE) negotiates wages and other related benefits with its employees (union/s) within the broad parameters laid down by the relevant administrative ministry and the Bureau of Public Enterprises (BPE). Once the management has negotiated a package with the union/s, it seeks the approval of the minister concerned and the BPE. Then the formal agreement between the management and the union/s is signed. In recent years, several PSEs have introduced productivity-linked incentive payment schemes, either under Section 31(A) of the Bonus Act or outside the framework of the Act. The act envisages the payment of a bonus linked with productivity, over and above the minimum statutory bonus. These days, there is also a growing feeling among the management of PSEs, that at least a part of the wages should be linked to performance, so as to improve the employee's motivation and the organization's efficiency, and hence, the performance of the Indian public sector.

In many PSEs, a part of the employee's remuneration is paid in the form of an incentive bonus, which is linked to the performance of the company. Productivity-based incentives are mostly given to groups (which are usually departments or sections). Each department has a well-defined target, which is based on equipment/machine capacity (production), techno-economic parameters (process cost), quality, and so on. Interestingly, some PSEs have started paying more and more attention to quality while measuring productivity.

The chairmen of many PSEs sign a memorandum of understanding (MOU) with the relevant administrative ministry. The MOU contains an agreement on a target output on a yearly basis. The chairman gives an assurance that the target will be achieved by the various units/departments/divisions of the company. To this end, he makes an annual performance plan, which is sometimes further divided into monthly targets and divisional/departmental targets. Performance rewards, incentive bonus and various allowances are attached to the achievement of the targets. These rewards are set by the company, and the structure of such schemes and the modalities of their operation are also discussed with the trade unions. Interestingly, in some cases, as in that of the Steel Authority of India Ltd (SAIL), though the incentive schemes are negotiated between the management and the trade unions, the management takes a unilateral decision on the matter. The reward schemes decided upon by the management are directly linked to the performance of the plant. We shall now proceed to review a few cases to understand the evolution of productivity bargaining as a process of introducing change in the Indian corporate sector.

Case 1: Steel Authority of India Ltd

The Steel Authority of India Ltd (SAIL), incorporated in 1973 from the erstwhile Hindustan Steel, is a leading public sector company with several manufacturing plants in India. Though SAIL has a large number of unions, only one union is recognized in one unit for the purpose of negotiation and collective bargaining. All major issues, including productivity, work practices, wages/bonus, technology and welfare, are discussed with the unions. On an average, the negotiations between the management and union are spread over 40–50 sittings, spanning two years. Only then is the deal finalized and the agreement with the unions signed. A wage increase of 15–20 per cent takes place after every settlement. The payment of a productivity-based incentive as part of the wages, which is not an uncommon practice in India, has been followed by SAIL too. The performance-based reward system is arrived at by identifying the thrust areas and linking the system to the departmental parameters. Discussions are held with the unions to agree upon a common approach. Once the system has been formally approved, it is communicated to all parties concerned and its implementation begins.

The incentive scheme, started in the 1960s, was related to the rated capacity of the department. The incentives varied on a point-to-point basis with variations in the production curve. However, important modifications were introduced in the scheme in 1986–87. This is when the company started signing a MOU with the government on a yearly basis. The chairman of SAIL now signs a MOU with the secretary of the department of steel. The MOU contains an agreement on the annual target of output. The chairman, in turn, signs annual performance plans (APPs) with the CEOs of the various individual companies (four separate companies) of SAIL, having reached an agreement on their respective targets. These targets would ultimately add up to the target agreed upon with the secretary of the department of steel. At the level of the plant, this annual target is further divided on a monthly basis.

Besides the APP, a reward scheme was also introduced in 1986–87. Nearly 60 per cent of the performance-based pay is given in the form of incentive, while 40 per cent is given as performance-based reward. In fact, since the introduction of the APP, the productivity incentive is calculated on a monthly basis. The monthly target is further subdivided into three to five blocks/slabs of targets, each block being linked to a fixed quantum of performance reward. For example, if the target is 100, the slabs may be fixed at 80, 90, 95 and 100.

In 1987–88, the government issued a guideline stating that not more than 35 per cent of the wage bill should be paid as incentive/variable pay. In 1995, it issued a clarification, saying that out of the 35 per cent, 20 per cent may be paid as annual bonus, which left only 15 per cent as variable pay. In fact, the upper limit of 35 per cent is applicable only to those PSEs which have signed a MOU with the government; the limit for other companies is just 30 per cent. Mostly, the productivity-based incentives are given to groups which are, by and large, departments or sections. Experiments with smaller groups within a section failed because of the high degree of interdependence between the employees of a department/section. Each department has a well-defined target, which is based on its equipment capacity. In fact, a department's equipment/machine capacity is laid down by the supplier of the machines/equipment, and this is normally not questioned.

In SAIL, production is linked to cost (process cost, which is termed a techno-economic parameter), on the one hand, and quality, on the other. Incentives are based on both the quality and quantity of production. The latter has been given a weightage of 90 per cent, though there were thoughts of raising the share of quality while measuring productivity. On the basis of this weightage, a Production Index (PI) is evolved and assigned as a percentage of the target fulfilled. Usually, PI figures range from 60 to 105. Correspondingly, a proportionate wage incentive, depending on the grade of the worker, is decided upon. There was variation in the quantum of incentive gain between the maximum and minimum to the extent of 1:4. Production shops were the basis where 90 per cent of the average amount could be paid. As for service departments, if they work for 48 hours or more a week, they can get a maximum of 50 per cent; if they work fewer hours, the percentage could be 40 per cent or less. The marketing department has a different method of calculation, which is based on the net sales realized. Within the production unit itself, there are variations in incentive between the primary zone (say, the coke ovens), and the finishing zone (say, the rolling mills). The latter earns higher incentives because of the use of better technology.

A unique feature of the reward scheme is that if the fixed target is not achieved, the entire amount earmarked as performance reward for that period is foregone by the department concerned. Moreover, the management takes a unilateral decision on the productivity-linked scheme, while the incentive scheme is negotiated jointly by the management and unions. In fact, no clause of the reward scheme is negotiable with the unions. Interestingly, if an employee has been charged with indiscipline, or has participated in a strike, he is not entitled to the performance reward during that period. It is odd that in the highly unionized environment of SAIL, this has never been questioned or challenged by the unions.

There are other allowances and incentive schemes for the managers and executives. These are linked to the performance of the plant and the utilization of the capacity of the plant. Officers up to the level of E-6 are given performance-linked incentive bonus, on the basis of the department's performance. Officers at the levels of E-7 to E-9 are given incentives on the basis of the global parameters, which are based on the overall performance of the plant.

Though the PSEs lack the freedom to evolve the pay structure which is directly linked with productivity, the private sector is increasingly negotiating pay systems that are directly linked to performance. This is true both of the domestic private sector and of multinationals. In the private sector at large, wages and other benefits are negotiated and settled between the management and employees (unions) through a process of collective (productivity) bargaining. This process culminates in the signing of a collective (productivity) agreement. In the event that the management and union/s are unable to reach an amicable settlement, third-party intervention is sought under the provisions of the Industries Disputes Act, 1947. This may take the form of conciliation, arbitration or adjudication. As the following cases show, the schemes introduced in the private sector—both domestic and multinational—are more directly linked to productivity than those in the public sector.

Case 2: Eicher Tractors Ltd

Eicher Tractors Ltd is a private sector company, which was established in 1976 at Mia in Rajasthan. This plant was meant for the manufacture of 24 HP tractor engines. Another plant was established in 1982 to manufacture 35 HP engines and tractors. Both plants became operational between 1983 and 1987, producing 24 and 35 HP engines and 35 HP tractors. In 1987–88, the operations of both plants were shifted to Alwar.

The management and the union at Eicher Tractors Ltd arrived at collective agreements on wages, working conditions and related issues, following discussions and negotiations. In 1994, the management entered into a three-year wage agreement with the union. According to the agreement, one part (75 per cent) of the pay was fixed and the other (25 per cent) was variable. At the same time, the management demanded a 36 per cent increase in productivity, to be achieved over a period of three years. The accompanying provision was that an employee could earn up to Rs 125 per month in the first year and another Rs 100 per month in the second year following the introduction of the new scheme. The scheme also included other modifications. The measurement of productivity, instead of being based on the total manpower of the plant, was now to be based on man days per unit (MDU). The latter was to be calculated according to given production lines. This method of calculation helped the company measure improvements in productivity more precisely. The scheme came into operation in 1994. By September 1997, productivity in the shops for single cylinder machines had improved by 60 per cent.

December 31, 1996 marked the beginning of a major chapter in the history of the company's industrial relations, in general, and productivity-linked wages scheme, in particular. The trade union, on behalf of the workmen, expressed a desire to give up the practice of negotiating a wage settlement. Instead, it proposed that the management should revise the workers' pay on an annual basis, the same way as the pay of the staff and executives was revised. They also opted out of the three-year wage settlement, a practice which had been prevalent till then. In response, the management initiated a new scheme, called the Engine Productivity, Quality and Attendance Scheme, on January 1, 1997. The scheme was applicable to all the permanent employees working in the company.

Eicher Tractors' scheme was the result of several years' efforts. The General Manager and his team had held several rounds of discussions with the union and its members since 1994. In the process, the management gained the confidence and trust of the workers. The management emphasized the fact that it would never say 'no' to a genuine request from the workers, but it would never agree to an unreasonable demand either. The management agreed that the workers would be better off without the prolonged process of negotiation, but it was not sure about how to implement the idea. Some of the union activists expressed apprehensions about the role they would be expected to play and the outcome of such a change. Some resisted the change, arguing that the new system would eliminate the trade union. However, the management insisted that the system would benefit both the workers and the company. The General Manager confided that 'ultimately, the management had to demonstrate that they meant business and that they knew what they were doing, at times just by being tough'. Once all fears were set aside, the scheme was finally launched. The results of the scheme have been encouraging. However, the process of reaching a meaningful agreement on productivity and wages need not always be easy, as the following case shows.

Case 3: Britannia Industries Ltd, Delhi

Incorporated in March 1918 in Calcutta as a public limited company, Britannia was the first company in the country to instal and run a gas oven plant for the manufacture of biscuits. Over the years, the company set up several factories in different parts of the country to provide bread, biscuits, seafood, and so on. In October 1979, the company's name was changed from Britannia Biscuits to Britannia Industries Ltd. In Britannia Industries Ltd, Delhi, wages and other issues relating to working conditions are discussed and negotiated by the management and the unions at regular intervals. The productivity-linked component of the wage is decided upon after undertaking industrial engineering studies, and the amount is finally settled through negotiations with the trade unions.

Though productivity was included in a wage settlement with the unions for the first time in 1990, it was only in a settlement made in 1994 that the link between productivity and wages was brought into sharper focus. On January 6, 1990, a comprehensive settlement covering all the terms and conditions of employment was signed between Britannia Industries Ltd and the two recognized unions (the Britannia Biscuit Company Mazdoor Union, affiliated to INTUC, and the Britannia Industries Karamchari Union, affiliated to CITU.) Under section 12(3) of the Industrial Disputes Act, 1947, the agreement was signed before the labour commissioner of the Delhi administration.

On December 17, 1992, the management received a charter of demands from the unions. The charter had been passed unanimously in the general body meeting of the workmen three days earlier. In response, the management attempted to explain in detail the constraints under which it was functioning. It told the workmen and their representatives that the company's economic viability was under threat due to the sharp increase in the prices of inputs, including labour. In addition, the demand for the product (bread) had become highly elastic as a result of decontrolling of bread by the government. Every price correction carried out by the company to balance the increased cost of inputs had resulted in a significant erosion of its market. Moreover, as the government had done away with price control, many other brands were available to the customer. The customer had naturally shifted loyalty to other brands charging lower prices, and this had considerably reduced the company's market share.

After explaining the rather critical situation of the company, the management submitted that any further increase in wages would necessarily have to be related to an increase in productivity from all resources, including labour. Wastage would have to be reduced and all restrictive practices eliminated. Though negotiations between the management and the union started in February 1993, a settlement was reached when the union raised the issue before the Conciliation Officer in November 1993. As the Britannia Industries factory at Lawrence Road (Delhi) was a public utility undertaking (it produced an essential commodity—bread), the Assistant Labour Commissioner/Conciliation Officer intervened almost immediately. A mutually acceptable settlement was signed by the unions and the management on February 2, 1994. It must be noted that the management was able to win the unions' approval for this settlement, which envisaged major changes in the work methods, technology, and so on.

The agreement notwithstanding, the trade unions resisted the idea of linking wages with productivity, and wanted only a small percentage of the wages to be linked to productivity. The practice of paying overtime was among the factors responsible for this. Another problem area was the fixing of standards and norms for measuring productivity, which is an elaborate and complex process. However, the management tried its best to make the settlement work. It had also initiated steps in the areas of human resource management and industrial relations. It is noteworthy that the management took all steps possible to maintain a healthy, if not completely harmonious, climate of industrial relations. As the new scenario urgently demanded the upgradation of technology, besides increased automation and productivity, the management realized that it was crucial for everyone to share and appreciate the company's goals. To this end, it decided to focus on training employees at all levels.

In fact, the management took major initiatives to train the workers, apart from training the officers and managers. The main step in this direction was to train all the workers under the aegis of the Central Institute for Workers' Education. The programmes were aimed at creating general awareness about liberalization, competitiveness and business plans, among the workers. The trade unions were initially opposed to such programmes and even tried to boycott them. In response, the management offered the trade union leaders themselves the opportunity to participate in training programmes aimed at helping them to develop leadership skills, and so on. These programmes were organised by the same institute. This training resulted in a change in the attitude of the union leaders. The major focus of the training programmes was on the quality of work life, improvement in productivity and attitudinal changes. The workers were provided with a record number of 1594 mandays of training in 1997.

After several rounds of discussions and negotiations, the management and unions arrived at a consensus on the revision of the incentive scheme in February 1998. The revised scheme would take effect from December 1, 1998. The objectives of the scheme were to (*a*) improve productivity by increasing the output, coupled with an improvement in the quality of production; (*b*) optimize the utilization of resources; (*c*) provide the workmen with a financial incentive for the additional efforts made by them; and (*d*) minimize, if not eliminate, the wastage of raw materials and finished products. The incentive scheme applied to all specified permanent/temporary workmen. Those working overtime would not be eligible for incentive earnings. The incentive would not be deemed to be a part of the wages for any purpose whatsoever. It did not attract dearness allowance, annual increment, provident fund, bonus, gratuity, overtime, and other benefits.

The workmen, represented by their unions, assured the company that they would not restrict the output in any manner, be it through unauthorized plant stoppages, go-slow, processions, demonstrations, *dharnas*, *gheraos*, work-to-rule, mass absence, refusal to work overtime when instructed to do so, or withdrawal from the workforce. The management and the workmen agreed to implement the terms of the settlement both in letter and in spirit. They undertook to fully co-operate with each other in the matter of maintaining discipline and a harmonious relationship, so as to facilitate an increase in productivity.

The workmen recognized the rights and responsibilities of the management. Thus, they appreciated the need to take every step to make the factory a viable unit. The workmen also agreed to cooperate with the company's moves to maintain and improve its business by introducing new machines. The management assured the workers that if they were rendered surplus as a result of the installation of machines, they would not be retrenched, but would be suitably redeployed. The management, on its part, submitted a charter of demands to the workers. The charter, which contained more than 50 items, dealt mostly with issues related to quality and productivity.

As mentioned earlier, the workmen agreed to maintain industrial peace during the period of the settlement, considering the benefits accruing to them.

The workmen also agreed not to resort to any direct action or any form of agitation on the issues covered by the terms of the settlement. It was understood between the two parties that *vide* the terms of the settlement, which was a package deal, all the demands contained in the workers' Charter of Demands, and all disputes, grievances and complaints of any nature whatsoever, stood fully and finally settled. The unions and the workmen agreed not to raise, pursue, agitate against, or be a party to any demand or dispute settled under the terms of the settlement. It was also agreed that they would not raise, pursue, or be a party to any demand or dispute that directly or indirectly involved any financial or other commitment made by the company while the settlement remained in force.

As for those workmen who did not want to be covered by this settlement, they would have the option of continuing under the terms and conditions of service that were applicable to them prior to the settlement. If they wanted to opt for the settlement they had to do so within 15 days of the date of the signing of the settlement. The benefits of the settlement were available only to those workmen who had accepted it as binding, and who had agreed to the terms and conditions of the settlement in writing. The management, however, reserved the right to grant refuse benefits of the settlement to workers who decided to opt for it after the stipulated 15 days. In this case, the benefits would be effective from a future date.

The case of Britannia Ltd amply demonstrates that major changes can be introduced in the work process, level of quality, and other improvements, through the process of negotiating a settlement with the employees (union). The settlement, which came at a time when the company was in a precarious position, helped to reduce costs and improve quality, the overall productivity and performance of the company.

Case 4: Hindustan Lever Limited

Hindustan Lever Ltd (HLL), one of the largest producers of synthetic detergents and soaps, was set up in October 1933 as Lever Brothers (India) Ltd. It had manufacturing plants in Bombay and Calcutta. In October 1956, the company was converted into a public limited company, with a reduction in the foreign equity holding. All the manufacturing and marketing activities carried out by Lever Brothers and Hindustan Vanaspati Manufacturing Company (a subsidiary of Unilever that manufacted Vanaspati), were taken over by Hindustan Lever after the amalgamation of the two companies.

Though the various plants under the umbrella of the HLL are governed by the overall policy of the company, the management of each plant enters into a negotiated settlement with the union/s of the respective area. We shall be discussing the case of the HLL plant at Khamgaon, which produces detergents and cosmetics. The management of this plant and the Hindustan Lever Kamagar Sangh signed an agreement on March 23, 1996, after a series of negotiations. An earlier settlement signed on January 2, 1992, had expired on October 31, 1995, and the union served a charter of demands one day before its expiry. Since bipartite negotiations had not led to an agreement, the union had sought the intervention of the Conciliation Officer on January 17, 1996. As a result, the March 1996 settlement was signed. This was to operate until October 31, 1999. The agreement covered all major issues, including technology, improvement in productivity and deployment of manpower.

The employees agreed to give their whole-hearted support to the management in the implementation of all the initiatives planned for achieving a world-class manufacturing status. The initiatives included steps for modernization, expansion, mechanization, and the rationalization of work methods/manpower deployment and systems at the Khamgaon factory/plants. The workers and union agreed to extend their full co-operation to the management in the matters of maintaining discipline, enhancing productivity and the quality of the various products (current as well as new ones) of the establishment.

Depending upon the exigencies of work, as decided by the management, the employees agreed to work in any section/operation of the Khamgaon establishment. They agreed to do whatever work was assigned to them at any point of time by their superior/s. Until the settlement remained in effect, they would not do anything or cause anything to be done that could disrupt the company's operations, or tarnish its image or that of its products. They undertook that for no month during the entire period of the settlement would they fail on account of causes/factors attributable to any of them. As for the daily-rated employees, they agreed to achieve a performance level above the Capacity Utilization Index (CUI) in order to be eligible for the group incentive scheme. The monthly-rated employees agreed to do the same to qualify for the factory performance allowance. The union and the management agreed to honour any other commitments made by them, either as part of the December 1988 or January 1992 agreements or otherwise, except those which had been modified by the new settlement.

According to the settlement, the employees' wages included fixed time rates, variable dearness allowance, fixed dearness allowance, house rent allowance, local conveyance allowance, social security allowance, attendance allowance, canteen cash subsidy allowance, deployment flexibility allowance, factory performance allowance, leave travel allowance, self-deployment allowance and washing allowance. The settlement laid special emphasis on the importance of linking wages to attendance, flexibility, factory performance and group productivity. As a first step towards arriving at productivity-linked wages, standards were established with the help of industrial engineering inputs and qualifiers were fixed. On the basis of these norms, pay-out amounts were also fixed.

The entire process was a participatory one, in which the employees were involved through their trade unions. The company discussed all issues relating to wages, productivity, technology, work practices, and so on, with the unions. The management constantly introduced innovations in the areas of human resources/industrial relations, including TPM, TQM, ISO and suggestion schemes. The HLL lays emphasis on continuous training and issues pertaining to human resource development, with the ultimate aim of serving its business needs.

Impact of Productivity-linked Wages

Though the productivity-linked wage schemes operating in various companies use different methods and modalities, they have all resulted in marked improvements in productivity, employee involvement and industrial relations. The schemes are better structured and monitored in companies belonging to the private sector (domestic and multinational), compared to those in the public sector. The same goes for the advantages and benefits derived/perceived by the employee.

A substantial improvement in industrial relations, in general, was reported in SAIL after the introduction of the performance-based reward scheme. The appraisal of individual performance was linked, though indirectly, to decisions regarding promotions and increments. If an employee was appraised as outstanding on a continuous basis for two to three years, he would be given more than one increment. SAIL followed a system of internal benchmarking, say between the different plants. In 1995-96, the company reported an overall improvement of 11–20 per cent in output, and an increase of about 11–20 per cent in the wage earnings of the workers. At the same time, it reported a reduction of 11–20 per cent in the cost of labour. Absenteeism declined by 5–10 per cent and manpower was reduced by 5–10 per cent.

According to the management of HLL, the introduction of productivity-linked wages had led to an increase in the output. Exact figures could not be supplied, primarily because no scientific system has been developed as yet for this purpose. According to the management, the employees' earnings had risen by 11–20 per cent. The cost of direct labour had gone down, though again, it was difficult to measure it in exact terms. There had been a reduction in manpower, but it was not possible to relate this directly to the scheme, as there could be many other possible reasons.

In 1995–96, Eicher Tractors Ltd reported an improvement of 21–30 per cent in output, and a 5–10 per cent reduction in the payment of overtime after the productivity-linked wages scheme was introduced. At the same time, the wage earnings of the workers rose by 20–30 per cent, while the cost of direct labour fell by 21–30 per cent. Absenteeism declined by 11–20 per cent and there was a substantial reduction also in the manpower employed by the company. Some other benefits of introducing productivity-linked wages are the elimination of casual employees; improvement in the systems for handling material; improvement in the lay-out; gradual/continuous introduction of low-cost automation to ease worker's fatigue and physical strain; and the growing desire to find new methods of working.

The new productivity-linked incentive scheme of Eicher Tractors Ltd was applicable only to direct labour engaged in production, and not to the staff or executives. According to the senior manager (manufacturing), the major factors motivating the workers were—the freedom to take initiatives, greater participation in decision making, and the improvement in the overall work environment and office facilities. As for the management, the major motivating factor, according to the General Manager, was the need to survive and hence, constantly improve productivity. The increased productivity of and profit made by the company as a whole were reflected in the fact that the staff and management did get an annual raise. The most important reason cited for the success of the scheme was the openness and trust that it had created between the management and workers. Because of this, there was a mutual willingness to accept the improvement of productivity as a shared responsibility and to work towards it. In the words of the General Manager of the plant, 'While industrial engineering and work-studies are important, the conviction and desire to improve are the most important factors in bringing about any change.'

Britannia Industries Ltd, finding itself amidst increased competition in the bread segment due to the intervention of trader commissions, started subcontracting the production of bread to smaller manufacturers. This was done under the close supervision of the management which also supplied the raw material to the smaller companies.

Manpower was rationalized, primarily through redeployment, in many areas of operation, including hygiene and maintenance. New plants and machinery were installed to produce new products. These included swissrolls, bread, cakes etc. The company also attempted to redeploy its manpower to raise profitability. Further, it introduced a scheme of voluntary separation of unfit and non-performing employees (by paying off some benefits, and so on). The company managed to restructure the organization to an extent by de-layering the number of workers' levels from five to three. This resulted in a reduction of manpower, with the company now having 93 less employees. The company reported an increase of about 41–50 per cent in output and a similar decline in the payment of overtime, as a result of the system introduced in 1994. The workers' wage earnings rose by 11–20 per cent and the cost of direct labour declined by a similar percentage; absenteeism went down by about 5 per cent, and manpower was reduced by more than 40 per cent.

Case 5: Larsen and Toubro, Bangalore Works

Productivity agreements of all types are intimately linked with the kind of industrial relations prevailing in the company. Cordial industrial relations are essential for facilitating the process of productivity bargaining on the basis of which productivity agreements are made. The case of Larsen and Toubro Ltd (L&T), Bangalore, is a good example of how a scheme may falter in the absence of congenial industrial relations.

Larsen and Toubro is a leading manufacturer and distributor of various types of machinery, equipment and services in India. The operations of the company were divided under 11 different groups, which dealt with a wide range of products and services. The Bangalore unit of L&T, which was established in 1975, comprised machinery works, hydraulic works and engine works. This unit, being a young organization, had a young workforce, too. The average age of the workforce was 28 years.

The first wage agreement with the workers of L&T was signed in 1976. Subsequently, the management negotiated long-term settlements with the L&T employees' union, affiliated to All-India Trade Union Congress (AITUC), every five years. According to the agreement of 1976, the management was to annually pay the workers a lump sum as *ex gratia* if the workers (*a*) maintained discipline and industrial peace, and had achieved the production target of the previous year; and (*b*) assured the management that they would maintain industrial peace and achieve the production target for the ensuing year. However, industrial relations at L&T became unstable due to the rising expectations of the young workforce and the increasing militancy of the unions in and around Bangalore during the 1980s. The workers disrupted work during 1982 and 1983, and resorted to a four-month long strike in 1984. On assurance from the union of industrial peace during the ensuing year, the management had made the *ex gratia* payment in 1982 and 1983. However, after the 1984 strike, the management decided that it would not do so again.

The concept of productivity-linked wages was introduced in 1985 for the first time. With the expiry of the preceding agreement in 1985, the management thought it appropriate to incorporate this concept as a part of the new long-term settlement which aimed at providing scope for higher earnings through the achievement of a level of production that exceeded the base output. The concept of productivity bargaining was also introduced, so that the base output would be gradually raised each year. In an agreement signed with the union in 1985, it was clearly emphasized that the employees' earnings would be linked with production and productivity. It was also agreed that the lump sum (*ex gratia*), paid annually earlier, would be paid in four quarterly instalments, subject to the achievement of the production target of the previous quarter. Thus, the *ex gratia* payment was converted into a post-performance reward. The union and workers accepted the proposal without hesitation, as the previous year's experience had shown that it was not difficult to achieve the target if industrial peace was maintained. However, industrial relations continued to be a source of trouble even after this agreement.

A memorandum of settlement signed on August 16, 1995, between the management and the union laid renewed emphasis on production and productivity. It was agreed that in addition to the basic wage, *ex gratia* would be paid in a lump sum to each employee who was confirmed or on probation, on the condition that he achieved the base output.

However, the implementation of productivity-linked wages was not a smooth process, in view of the company's history of disturbed industrial relations. Soon after the settlement of 1995, factional divisions within the union led to a change in its leadership. The newly elected union leaders argued that the management had forced the conditions of the agreement on the workers. They refused to accept the norms which had been worked out by the industrial engineers and had later been agreed upon by the previous leadership. They went on a strike, following which, the management declared a lock-out. The matter was then referred for adjudication.

The new leadership of the union also resented the move towards multi-skilled workers, which was gradually becoming more marked with the introduction of new technologies. According to an officer of the human resources department, the reason for L&T's lack of success in introducing the system of productivity-linked wages was that sufficient attention was not paid to the entire gamut of human resource management. Thus, the piecemeal approach to productivity-linked wages could not succeed.

Conclusion: Productivity Bargaining and Change

The inception of productivity bargaining is closely associated with change. Further, once introduced, productivity bargaining continues to be an important mechanism whereby the management and union (employees) can evolve a consensus on the implementation of mutually beneficial changes in the workplace. In post-liberalized India, the management was able to introduce changes in technology, work methods, manpower deployment, and so on, in companies which signed agreements linking wages with productivity. The case studies described in this chapter amply illustrate this. While companies in the private sector have met with greater success in this respect, those in the public sector, too, have developed a system of bilateral negotiations for determining the wages and benefits of the employees, as illustrated by the case of SAIL, for example. Similarly, the National Thermal Power Corporation (NTPC) has evolved schemes to measure performance and for linking earnings to performance. The corporation set predetermined targets and dates for their achievement, and the quantum of pay would vary according to the actual date of achieving the targets. It was observed that performance-based pay provided the employees with enough motivation to even achieve the targets ahead of schedule. In the Indian Oil Corporation, another public sector undertaking, 15 per cent of the pay was linked to productivity. This portion was paid as productivity incentive. The NTPC reported an improvement of as much as 11–20 per cent in output and a similar increase in the wage earnings of the workers. In the cases of both SAIL and NTPC, productivity-linked wage systems have had a positive impact on industrial relations and the level of motivation among the employees.

As mentioned already, companies in the private sector have developed and implemented productivity-linked wage systems with more satisfactory results. In fact, in Eicher Tractors Ltd, productivity was reported to have improved much beyond the agreed target. Similarly, the management and union of the Indian Tobacco Company (ITC), Kidderpore, signed an agreement according to which the workers would be paid productivity-linked wages, with the wages being based on a 'productivity index plan'. The management prepares this plan. Another company operating a productivity-linked incentive scheme is RPG Telecom Ltd. The plan is based on the plant's overall performance, which is measured in terms of the quality and quantity of output. It is calculated on a monthly basis. The schemes introduced by both ITC and RPG have had positive results.

We have already noted that productivity-linked wages are more prevalent in multinational and (domestic) private sector enterprises than in the public sector. This may be explained by the fact that international experience has helped the MNCs develop better systems of productivity-linked wages. Those enterprises in the (domestic) private sector which are more professionally managed and competitive are not far behind. As the wages of employees in the public sector continue to be determined by government-appointed commissions/boards at the central level, individual enterprises do not have much scope to negotiate wages. Until and unless the management of public sector undertakings are given greater autonomy to determine the wages and benefits of the employees, the introduction of productivity-linked wage schemes may yield only limited results.

On the basis of the cases discussed in this chapter, we can sum up the issue by making two important observations. One, in recent years, companies in India have been able to use the process of productivity bargaining as an effective mechanism to bring about successful changes in the workplace. Two, productivity bargaining and productivity-linked wage schemes however, cannot succeed unless accompanied by other innovations in the areas of human resource management and industrial relations.

References

Ahmed, M. U. (1997). Productivity-linked Wages in Bangladesh. New Delhi: ILO Report (unpublished).

Asian Productivity Organization. (1994). *Linking Wages with Productivity.* Tokyo; Asian Productivity Organization: Monograph Series, 5.

Dasanayaka, G.K.B. (1997). Productivity-linked wages in Sri Lanka. New Delhi: ILO Report (unpublished).

Dong, T. J. (1994). Flexible wage system: The Singapore experience. Tokyo; Asian Productivity Organization, Monograph Series, 5.

Inouye, S. (1994). Productivity gain-sharing systems: Japanese experience. In *Linking Wages with Productivity.* Asian Productivity Organization: Monograph Series, 5.

Flanders, A. (ed). (1969). *Collective Bargaining.* Harmondsworth: Penguin.

International Labour Office (1997). *World Labour Report, 1997–98.* Geneva: International Labour Office.

Mamkoottam, K. (1997). Productivity-linked Wages in India. New Delhi: ILO Report (unpublished).

North, D.T.B. and **Buckingham, G. L.** (1969). *Productivity Agreements and Wage Systems.* London: Gower Press.

Pandey, N. K. (1997). *Productivity-linked Wages in Nepal.* New Delhi: ILO Report (unpublished).

Shaheed, Z. (1994). Some general trends in relating pay to productivity in Western European countries. Tokyo: Asian Productivity Organization, Monograph Series, 5.

Siddiqqi, F. K. (1997). *Productivity-linked Wages in Pakistan.* New Delhi: ILO Report (unpublished).

Suri, G.K. (1976). *Productivity, Wages and Industrial Relations.* New Delhi: Affiliated East–West Press Pvt. Ltd.

Venu, M.K. (1999). 'PSUs take to slimming...' *The Economic Times,* June 1.

6

Change and Industrial Relations*

As discussed in the previous chapters, the increasingly competitive environment in recent years has necessitated the adoption of new technologies by organizations. The rather slow response of the Indian industrial sector to technological innovation, as well as its indifference to introducing new products and reorganizing work, have often been attributed to the industrial relations scenario in the country. Labour and trade unions have had a negative and non co-operative attitude in India. In fact, the literature shows that labour and trade unions have adopted a similar stance to technological innovation and change even elsewhere in the world. The three exceptions are Japan, the Scandinavian countries and Germany. In general, the management takes the initiative to introduce technological changes to improve the work process, while labour takes a reactive position. Technological change has remained primarily the concern of the management, to which raising the levels of productivity, efficiency and profitability are of primary importance. The more positive approach of the unions and labour to technological change in Japan may be attributed to the corporate paternalism characterizing industrial relations in the country. In the cases of Germany and the Scandinavian countries, the pattern of co-determination can be said to have been of great use. These countries adopt a more process-oriented approach to industrial relations, which are characterised by a positive and collaborative approach.

In general, the trade unions and labour have supported technological change and automation at the workplace only to the

---

* Many of the international experiences referred to in this chapter are based on an ILO paper entitled, 'Labour institutions and technological change: A framework for analysis and a review of the literature' (2000).

extent that the changes did not cost them their jobs. However, the recent technological developments have been of such a radical nature that organized labour has had to rethink its reactive strategy. The increased competitiveness of the global market, with its attendant demands for greater flexibility and efficiency, has complicated the relationships between labour, the management and the process of technological change. This chapter deals with certain aspects of industrial relations and the process of change, and the role of the worker and trade unions in introducing change, with particular reference to the adoption of new technologies.

It is believed that the history and structure of industrial relations—both at the national and enterprise levels—influence the strategy of labour and trade unions to technological change (Davis and Lansbury, 1987; Ozaki, 1992). Although theoretically, there is an emerging consensus among the trade union leaders and political parties on the need to develop collaborative industrial relations, empirical evidence mostly shows that labour's approach to technological change has not changed much. Although the trade unions have generally become more co-operative, the new balance between co-operation and confrontation has not significantly altered the trade unions' stance on technological change.

International experience shows that the interface between labour relations and technological change may produce two forms of co-operation. In the first kind, co-operation arises in an atmosphere of adversarial industrial relations. In most cases, the initiation of a process of change by the management creates further pressure for co-operation. In the second kind of scenario, both the management and labour seek to reduce the perceived threats presented by the process of change. The management sees this threat in terms of the inefficiency arising from labour's resistance to change; and labour sees it in terms of the negative impact of change (and new technology) on the levels of skill and employment. It must be noted that such co-operation is characterized by a low level of participation by labour in the change process.

The second kind of co-operation grows out of a history of cordial industrial relations which help expand the scope of discussion from distributive to process-oriented issues. Here, the emphasis is on the management of human resources, who are seen in terms of an investment, and whose co-operation and involvement are necessary for achieving the organization's goals. This is further reinforced by a more user-based design for change, a design which recognizes the need to integrate human and technical factors while effecting change. In this form of co-operation, the level of mutual interests (which are clearly defined) is relatively high. This encourages both the management and labour to work towards enhancing productivity and competitiveness, and thereby, job security. These goals are accomplished by efforts to incorporate the experiential (tacit) knowledge of labour into the change process. Such co-operation is characterized by intense involvement on the part of the employee. It takes the form of negotiation, joint decision making and joint formulation of strategies.

As Sorge and Streeck (1988) suggest, technology, including IT and microelectronics, is not deterministic enough to transform the workplace in a predetermined manner. In fact, it is the existing climate of industrial relations and the organization's decision-making process that produce the technology's impact on the workplace. Often, an adversarial industrial relations environment results in resistance to the management's initiatives, as the level of trust between the management and labour is low. It has been observed that labour is more co-operative in a low-risk situation, i.e., a situation which requires a minimum of organizational restructuring, and in which the impact on employment or occupational structures is marginal. In this situation, co-operation is meant to overcome the potential negative impact of the process of change; it should be seen as just a small element in the evolution of a better climate of industrial relations.

On the other hand, co-operation which has been developed on the basis of collaborative decision making sustains itself. This is because of the presence of a well-defined set of mutual interests. This is the type of co-operation which has characterized industrial relations in the Scandinavian countries, Germany and Japan for a long time. In recent years, many other countries, including the US and some European nations, have tried to import innovative practices of human resource management from Japan, Germany and the Scandinavian countries. There is a growing trend towards a more co-operative approach to decision making and problem solving.

The environment of industrial relations in India has been dominated by an adversarial model for a long time, though a gradual shift is beginning to take place towards a more collaborative model. In an earlier chapter, we have discussed several efforts to sign productivity agreements in order to facilitate the process of change. These agreements often also covered technological change and reorganization of work, although the choices regarding innovations and technologies may have remained largely with the management. However, some such agreements were also accompanied by collaborative industrial relations and progressive practices of human resource management, as in the case of Eicher Tractors.

Change and the Climate of Industrial Relations

As we have been saying, organizational change, in general, and technological innovation, in particular, must be analyzed within the context of the climate of industrial relations—both national and enterprise-specific—within which they are attempted. Laws pertaining to industrial relations and bilateral collective agreements are intended to create an 'enabling framework', within which enterprises should be able to develop a co-operative work atmosphere. As discussed already, industrial relations in India have been controlled by state regulation for a long time. Collective bargaining and bilateral negotiations have been a rare phenomenon, though these practices are gradually gaining popularity in recent years. A plethora of labour laws regulate wages/monetary benefits, the minimum standards of employment and social security. They also provide a framework for the prevention and resolution of industrial disputes.

All parties concerned have recognized that such legislative measures have met with limited success, and at times, have even hindered the development of a more collaborative system of industrial relations. None of the affected parties, including the employer, employee and trade unions, has found the legislative framework, especially the administration and implementation of labour laws, satisfactory. Though these laws were well-intended, they mainly serve to form a framework within which enterprises can evolve certain limited industrial relations practices. At best, these laws provide a framework for some kind of involuntary co-operation, by stipulating the need for 'notification' and attempting to restrain the employer and worker's freedom to resort to direct action. The prevailing legal framework aside, collective bargaining has not yet reached any significant level of acceptability in India. A climate of meaningful co-operation can be developed only by an open-minded management, which believes in a progressive system of managing human resources and a proactive strategy of industrial relations, supported by forward-looking labour/unions.

Cross-national surveys and case studies from other countries illustrate that the speed and nature of change, especially the introduction of new technologies, are influenced by the climate of industrial relations. Various studies on technological change in Europe (EFILWC, 1987; Gill and Krieger, 1992; Mamkoottam and Herbolzeimer, 1991) show a close relationship between technological change and the prevailing industrial relations culture. The EFILWC study, based on 64 case studies and an attitudinal survey of 7326 respondents chosen from each member-country of the European Community, shows that forms of co-operation on new technology vary and are, to a large extent, a product of the different cultures of industrial relations in different countries. Gill and Krieger (1992) conclude that the levels of participation across different countries in the EC are largely shaped by the historical and cultural features characterizing the industrial relations system in the particular country.

The historical and cultural features include, though are not limited to, national legislation and collective bargaining (agreements). The Swedish and Norwegian models provide the most mature examples of participatory industrial relations being facilitated by national legislation.

In these models, legislation is used to create an 'enabling framework' for the trade unions. The legislation contains provisions for retraining of employees and security of employment, both of which soften the impact of technical change on the workforce. These provisions thus encourage proactive dialogue at an early stage in the planning and designing of technological innovation (Cressey, 1991a). Empirical studies from Sweden show that the process of change is often spurred on by inputs from the worker (Ozaki, 1992). This is a clear example of how the culture of industrial relations in a particular country, as well as the type of legislation it gives rise to, can facilitate the elaboration of models of strategic cooperation between labour and the management. Similarly, the Japanese pattern of 'corporate paternalism' offers its workers job security. The sense of 'mutuality of interests' is so highly developed that the Japanese do not need to resort to legislation for labour and the management to co-operate on technological change and innovation.

National legislation alone cannot create co-operation at the enterprise level. The German model of co-determination grew out of a unique history of linkages between work relations, training at the workplace, and the provision of formal education by the state. Under the model of co-determination, workers play a significant role in making decisions related to new technology. However, several other EC countries which attempted to introduce legislation modelled on the German example, have not met with the same success. In France and Belgium, for example, legislation enacted to make industrial relations more participatory, has shown the limitations of the legislative mechanism. It has not always been able to encourage a dialogue between the employers and workers (Tallard, 1988; Alberton et al., 1990). The nature, complexity and subtlety of new technologies, are such that it is often difficult to implement them strictly through legislation. Legislative standards pertaining to employment and work content are difficult to enforce from a distance. Further, in order to pass such legislation, it may become necessary to establish a direct correlation between the implementation of new technology and employment. The process of establishing such a direct linkage has become increasingly difficult as the new technologies are inherently flexible and depend less and less on human intervention. In India, too, the laws enacted to regulate employer–employee relations, and to prevent and resolve industrial disputes, have not proved effective at all in the current context.

While governments have pursued legislation, trade unions have attempted to influence the workplace through collective bargaining (agreements). In response to the recession of the late 1970s in the UK, the Trade Union Commission prepared a report, outlining the conditions for union negotiation of New Technology Agreements (Beirne and Ramsay, 1992). The 1979 Employment and Technology Report encouraged the unions to adopt a very proactive approach to the subject of new technology, and recommended conditions for the implementation of such technology. The report including a 10-point check-list, covered issues such as job security, health and safety, and training. In addition, it attempted to expand the scope of trade union involvement, calling for greater worker participation in the designing and choice of new technology (Simpson et al., 1987).

Unfortunately, there has been no such understanding or agreement at the national level in India, although the new industrial Policy announced in 1991 had broadly envisaged various clauses relating to structural adjustments, particularly through the provisions of the National Renewal Fund. The fact remains that such agreements have been signed only at the local level, within individual enterprises. These local agreements have had only a limited impact on the corporate sector as a whole, perhaps because there has been little or no direct involvement of the employees in such cases. The main purpose of these agreements has been to overcome the workers' (and union's) resistance to change by providing them with information on the inevitability of technological change and also by highlighting the immediate benefits accruing to them. This too has been done in a limited manner. More often than not, technical innovation is considered to be an 'economic concern' and thus, the decision 'to implement' or 'not to implement' is seen as being within the discretion of the employer. In some of the productivity agreements signed in India, the management has been placed under no obligation to share its decision-making authority with the employees/unions. It is a different matter that the management has agreed to communicate certain information, or at least consults the employees in advance in some cases.

Change at the Level of Enterprises

The real impact of change is experienced at the level of individual enterprises. Real change takes place when employees at all levels of an organization accept the reasons, process and consequences of change. In other words, the involvement and participation of employees at all levels is essential to ensure the success of the process of change. It is now being recognized that for such involvement to be forthcoming, the employees have to develop a sense of ownership within the organization. This is all the more so because technological changes and other processes relating to strategy require a high degree of trust between the actors involved. All parties concerned need to appreciate that these changes would be in their mutual interest. Incorporating the workers' interests into the process significantly alters the established network of concerns and issues being addressed. As discussed earlier, the degree to which the history of industrial relations has been defined by confrontation or the search for a mutuality of interests, is an important factor in determining the model of co-operation to be pursued. In most cases, the management pursues technological innovations, while the unions use the collective bargaining process to negotiate a 'price for change'. The prime concern of the latter is to minimize the impact of new technology on the conditions of work. The unions are less concerned with the more process-oriented questions of when and how to influence the process of introducing new technology.

More often than not, it is the management which chooses the strategies for change, including technological innovation. It also sets the rules and decides the extent to which the workers and unions should be involved. While deciding on the introduction of new technologies, the choice of strategies available to the management is dictated, to a large extent, by the firm's history of industrial relations, on the one hand, and its recent experience with the implementation of new technology, on the other. There is a greater possibility of holding a meaningful dialogue with the employees when the history has been one of positive collaboration, trust and well-defined mutual interests. In recent years, many attempts in India have failed primarily because there was little or no understanding between the management and the labour/unions on the objectives of and the gains/losses arising from technological changes.

The level of unionization and the skills of the workforce are other important factors that influence industrial relations and the propensity to accept change. Since both these factors play an important role in defining the character of industrial relations in a firm, they are also important determinants of the degree of readiness to accept the process of technical innovation. A union's traditional role of acting as the 'voice' of the employees is critical in creating production systems which are more quality-driven, and require higher levels of skills among the workers, as well as a better level of communication between the workers and managers. Under the pressures of heightened global competition and the increasingly complex technology, there has been a gradual decline in the trade unions' resistance to technological change. Perhaps for the same reason, we find that it is often easier to introduce technological changes in the high-skilled sectors, such as the IT industry and telecommunications.

In the face of the growing competitiveness and the search for greater commitment from the employees, enterprises are turning to newer methods, such as Employee Stock Ownership Programmes (ESOPs), to improve productivity and the quality of work. This trend may be seen as a part of the larger need to revitalize the workplace by focusing on more co-operative forms of management, information-sharing and problem-solving. The goal of such methods is to create a company in which everyone acts like an owner (Case, 1993). There are other gain-sharing initiatives (like the ESOP), too, which aim to establish a new corporate culture. Although improved industrial relations are assumed to be an outcome of ESOPs, analyses of ESOPs show that ownership and gain-sharing initiatives alone do not bring about increases in productivity or profitability (Rosen, 1992). Rather, ownership (participation in economic returns) has its greatest impact when linked to participation in decision making (Levine and Tyson, 1990; Jones, 1992). Therefore, better climate of industrial relations can serve as a springboard for the elaboration of participatory strategies with the consequent involvement of the employees. Employees who would be able to use their particular competencies and skills, would have a positive effect on the processes of technological innovation and change.

Industrial Relations and Innovative Strategies

Gann and Senker (1993) have observed significant differences between the innovative strategies pursued by firms in Japan and those pursued in the West or other parts of the world. There are striking differences in their respective goals, as well as in the quality of the innovation process itself. The robots used in the UK and the US are often very sophisticated machines, which are developed in isolation in advanced conditions. Their purpose is to minimize human intervention in the production process, and to achieve a quantum leap in the automation of production. In Japan, on the other hand, the robots are much simpler. They are primarily single-task machines, which serve to ease the repetitiveness of specific tasks. The use of robots in Japan has brought about a slight increase in the levels of automation, but the robots help achieve greater productivity nonetheless, as they incorporate a significant amount of the workers' existing knowledge.

The integration of both technological and human concerns in the innovation process is seen as a major factor contributing to Japan's success in 'low-cost flexible production'. Such integration enables the system to achieve high levels of productivity with relatively less complex machinery. The Japanese production process is considered a unique one, in which skilled workers and machines complement each other. The Japanese innovation strategy has been cited as an example of the 'socio-technical theory'. It is seen as a case in which joint optimization of organization and technology require a less than optimum state in each element by itself. The differences between the patterns of technological innovation in Japan and those in other countries have been attributed to the fact that their respective strategies of innovation have different goals (Tidd, 1991; Gann and Senker, 1993).

In labour-surplus markets like India, where the levels of unemployment are alarmingly high and those of quality and productivity abysmally low, the purpose and effects of technological innovations/change are often contradictory in nature. The management, labour and the state do not always perceive them in the same way, and such differences in perception make the process of change relatively more difficult. In addition, the inherent complexity of technological change, besides the workers'/unions' lack of experience and technical resources, often inhibit the process of meaningful participation by the worker. The productivity agreements signed at HLL and Eicher Tractors Ltd are both considered successful examples of the introduction of technological change through productivity bargaining. However, the workers representatives in the bargaining committee, which also discussed and decided upon technological changes, were the representatives of unions, who may not have had sufficient knowledge to address technical issues.

Lansbury et al. (1992) have compared participatory approaches used in Swedish and Australian plants in the automotive components industry. They felt that the Australian plant was characterized by the most negative features of industrial relations. It was the site of a large number of unions, that too, with overlapping coverage. The number of disputes over job classification and organization was also high. The Swedish plant, though not considered to be an example of best practice, had been functioning according to systems of joint consultation and team development for years. In the Australian plant, even though industrial relations were improving, the extent of the workers' involvement was limited. They were merely supplied with information and were consulted only after the management had taken the decisions. In contrast, the Swedish plant had encouraged joint decision making very frequently while initiating far-reaching activities for reorganization.

Those considering the development of a participatory model must recognize that labour unions, in particular, have an important role to play in ensuring the success of innovative changes. Trade unions can play a valuable role in helping to reorganize the workplace by monitoring and moderating the reorganization of work, the pay/reward systems (including job security), and the upgradation of knowledge and skills of the workforce.

The impact of technological change on the workforce depends on the management's intentions while introducing innovations, on the one hand, and the trade unions' response to such changes, on the other. In general, the management introduces technological changes primarily to increase competitiveness, either by lowering costs and/or enhancing the price: performance ratio (Sabel, 1993). Though the trade unions have traditionally been preoccupied with distributive concerns (such as wages and benefits), the new technological and market compulsions, combined with the new strategies of the management, have added new pressures—pushing them to re-examine their role. They now have to consider expanding their domain, and are beginning to turn their attention to areas like technological change and the upgradation of knowledge.

In sum, it is the co-operative model of indusrial relations that has facilitated innovative changes. The management and labour in most countries, with the exception of a few newly industrialized countries) NICs, are beginning to adopt the strategy of co-operation. It is now widely recognized that the involvement of workers benefits all parties concerned. Ozaki (1992) stresses the importance of the context in which the models of worker participation are evolved. He notes that the existing organization of work and structure of skills play a significant role in the success of initiatives meant to involve the worker. For example, in Sweden, Germany and Japan, jobs have historically been defined flexibly and the workers (or work teams) have been given relatively high degree of autonomy. In the US, the UK, France and Italy, job classifications are more rigid, and the relationship between the management and labour more adversarial. India, too, belongs to the latter category. These traditions shape the nature of worker participation, as also the effects of such participation, particularly in the processes used for selecting and adapting technological changes.

The development of a collaborative model of industrial relations requires fundamental changes in the attitudes of all the actors involved—the workers, labour leadership and management. In most successful cases of collaboration, due importance has been assigned to job security during the process of change. Another important factor is the introduction of programmes for training and retraining. In fact, much of the literature confirms the observation that it is in the area of training that labour institutions participate the most actively and successfully (Ozaki, 1992; Brown, Reich and Stern, 1993).

Technological Change and Trade Unions

As we have discussed earlier, new technologies pose special challenges, and sometimes a major threat, to trade unions. Technological change often reduces the size of the unions and blurs the traditional demarcations between them. In a study of unions in Finland, Koistinen and Lilja (1988) describe the ways in which technology challenges the unions' traditional procedures regarding job security and job classification. Their findings show that new technology can catalyze fundamental changes in the norms and values of trade unions. They describe situations in which young semi-skilled workers have received training in new technology. The training most often enhances their prestige, but also conflicts with the unions' traditional procedures, according to which prestige is determined largely by seniority.

We have also discussed that the leadership of the trade unions should adopt more proactive strategies, as against the reactive approach which has been followed for decades. While it is natural for them to be concerned about the potential loss of jobs and the growing obsolescence of manpower in the immediate future, it is also important that they assess the consequences of not adopting new technologies. These should be assessed specifically in the context of competitiveness and the generation of employment. Unions which choose to continue with the adversarial tradition are often found floundering in confusion, or hampered by various constraints including organizational and technical expertise to manage the period of transition.

Our examination of the examples of Japan, Sweden and Germany has shown us that the dynamics of labour–management relations in these countries involve permanent innovation and strategic action from both parties. Several authors have attempted to describe the components of such a partnership. According to Marshall (1992), for example, the central features of production systems with superior performance levels depend on the proper management of human resources, the enhancement of quality and productivity, and flexibility on the part of all actors. He also mentions larger and more frequent flows of information, ample learning opportunities and democratic participation. Brown, Reich and Stern (1993) developed the security, employee involvement and training (SET) model, which lays emphasis on the interrelation between job security, training and employee involvement. According to the model, such an interrelation enhances productvity, quality and competitiveness. Also, the employees become more interested in their work and have more to offer.

Kuwahara's (1992) description of the labour–management dynamics in Japan supports the SET model. Kuwahara dwells on the centrality of labour concerns, such as job security and training. According to him, as long as the idea of lifetime employment continues to be vitally important in Japan, the success or failure of an enterprise will greatly affect the lives of its employees. Innovative firms have advantages over those which are not progressive, one being their attractiveness to the workers. In addition, the preponderance of enterprise unions, especially in small to middle-sized firms, has greatly facilitated the maintenance of this co-operative dynamic. In a research conducted by the Japan Institute of Labour, the basic approach of the unions towards technological innovation has been described as being one of 'conditional approval' (Japan Institute of Labour, 1985). The conditions for approval are: (*a*) the demonstrated ability of new information technology (NIT) to help the company and facilitate the 'progress of human society'; (*b*) that the unions be consulted before the firm makes the decisions; and (*c*) job security, maintenance of good working conditions, and reduction of the workload and dangerous work, rather than reduction of labour.

According to Ozaki (1992), unions in Germany have displayed a critical, but constructive attitude to NIT. This constructive attitude is actually helping the unions and work councils transform and strengthen their role in the introduction and adaptation of NIT. They have begun taking a closer look at their structure and the composition of their membership. This should ultimately help revitalize the work council into an institution that truly acts in co-determination with the management, in the specific context of NIT.

As mentioned earlier, the nature of trade unionism in the US has largely been determined by a strong adversarial tradition, established during the 1930s and 1940s. The labour unions there exemplify the attitude of 'negotiating a price for change' (McLoughlin and Clark, 1988). Their primary concerns are to retain as many jobs as possible and to maintain job security measures for those who remain employed. This limited approach is increasingly meeting with failure, and has mostly resulted in significant job losses and substantial reductions in wages. In the process, labour unions in the US seem to have lost their appeal, considering the dramatic decline in union density. Recent events, however, indicate some movement towards more co-operative industrial relations. Scannell (1993) gives us an instructive description of the International Bakery, Confectionery and Tobacco Workers' Union (BC&T). Heeding the clear warning signs, the union, on its own initiative, took several proactive steps to identify strategies for the future of the workers in the industry. It set up a technology task force, which conducted an extensive survey of the conditions prevailing in the industry, reviewed the literature available, and carried out visits and interviews at the work sites. The task force finally drafted a policy on technology and decided upon a course of action. Its recommended that reorganization of the workplace should be allowed to continue, and that the direction of reorganization should be determined and controlled with the help of the union. It recommended that technology representatives be chosen from among the union's members. These representatives would try to ensure that the union was given opportunities to participate in the change process from the early stages. They would also seek involvement in the development of information databases on technology and would provide technical assistance. Similarly, unions in the telecom sector in India, including the state-controlled MTNL, have recently started supporting the introduction of new technologies, but on the condition that it should not cause loss of jobs, retrenchment of the existing employees or privatization.

Clausen and Lorentzen (1993), using data from a study of small companies which employ between 80 and 600 workers, describe how labour unions in the metal working industry in Denmark and Sweden promote new ways of organizing work. They have been involved in setting operators and setters in work schedules, planning tasks, and introducing the use of sequential time structures in the case of simultaneous performance of multiple tasks. The proactive stance adopted by the Swedish and Danish unions is due, in part, to a comprehensive structural rationalization, which has extended ownership so that it covers a certain proportion of the workforce. The workers and their representatives have a greater in-depth understanding of the ways in which new ways of organizing work can affect productivity and thereby, profitability.

Similarly, Ozaki (1992) reports that at a printing company in Germany, the introduction of NIT required a transition from a single-shift to a three-shift workday. The details of this rescheduling were worked out through joint consultation between the management and labour. Industrial relations in Japan replicate many of the dynamics of co-operation that can be observed in the northern European countries. Since many of the unions are enterprise unions and have a long (more than 40 years) history of collaboration with the management, decisions on NIT and its implementation are made jointly, in the first case, and gradually, in the second. Interestingly, the gradual introduction of NIT in some cases means that NIT operates alongside much older forms of production. Thus, the workforce is divided according to seniority and people are assigned jobs according to the technical or physical requirements for manipulating the production process (Kuwahara, 1992).

In addition, since lifetime employment is the norm in the larger Japanese corporations, the issues of job security and wages are not as contentious for Japanese workers as they are for workers in other countries, particularly those in India and the US. For example, the introduction of robots in the Japanese auto industry did not result in a fall in the employees' wages, regardless of whether or not the worker was reassigned to a new division or job classification (Japan Institute of Labour, 1985). In order to deal with the lower requirement of workers resulting from the introduction of NIT, Japanese companies often slow down their recruitments rather than displace employees. Sometimes, the practice of early retirement is used. Another strategy used in Japanese companies is that of shifting workers (through self-selection and providing training) into sales work. This serves a useful purpose because these workers can now concentrate on expanding the firm's markets, which partly serves to compensate for the increased productivity that follows the introduction of NIT.

Labour unions and works councils in Germany, too, have been successful in setting the management to include important pay/ reward provisions in their agreements. The introduction of numerically controlled production technology raised certain problems regarding the wages of workers. The management and works councils, with some guidance from the union leadership, reached an agreement on a policy, which guaranteed no lay-offs and no downgrading of positions despite the introducion of this new process (Ozaki 1992). Workers in a newspaper firm in Italy achieved similar provisions for job security, with the assistance of the labour union. In this case, NIT was being introduced in photocomposition, but it was guaranteed that no worker would be displaced. Instead, the workers who opted for early retirement were given assistance in finding new jobs in other companies. Others were able to shift to other departments within the company, following minimal training.

Training and Co-operative Industrial Relations

In most parts of the world, it is in the area of training that the unions and management have been able to work together successfully in order to make new technology workable. Some of the European countries provide the best instances of labour collaborating with the management in the area of training for new technology. In Denmark and Sweden, the 1980s ushered in a new era of consensus between labour and management. In these two countries, labour institutions in the metal working industries opted for educating the workers by enrolling them in vocational schools. These schools offered training programmes meant to help promote integration with NIT (Clausen and Lorentzen, 1993). The Works Constitution Act in Germany gives work councils the right to participate in decisions on training curricula in the firm. It also allows for their involvement in the introduction of new equipment and the designing of training meant for its use, and training pursued outside the firm.

Deutsch (1987) describes the efforts of IAM workers at the US Naval Research Laboratory, where training programmes were made available through a local community college. The training focused on the provision of skills for programming numerical control machines. In addition, the IAM advocated a 'train the trainer' approach. According to this, the employees are actually designated trainers and thus, are always available to train other workers. This naturally helps build in-house capacity. Finally, the IAM added technology training to the curriculum of its national education centre. This training is especially targeted at the union officials, so that they can respond effectively to the introduction of NIT.

Deutsch also highlights the substantial efforts made by the UAW, and the union's dealings with both the Ford Motor Company (Ford) and General Motors (GM). The union signed contracts with both companies in 1982. According to these, the employers were to help establish training and development centres by contributing 5 cents per hour. The contributions amounted to $10 million in the case of For and $ 40 million in that of GM. The training centres established offer courses which are specifically targeted to employees who have been displaced or affected by the introduction of NIT.

There have been a few exemplary efforts to train employees in the telecommunications industry as well. AT&T and the Bell companies associated with it initiated a training programme, which is overseen by the CWA. Mostly, the training is provided in the form of courses offered by community colleges and vocational schools. There is also an assortment of home study programmes. These courses offer the employees career counselling, improve their basic literacy skills, and train them to operate with NIT. Scannell's 1993 study documents the recommendations for training made by a BC&T task force. These include the development of worker education programmes to disseminate information about the training programmes available for NIT, the unions' position on technology, the progress made in bargaining efforts concerning the adaptation of technology, organization of the workplace, and so on.

Jain (1992) documents the efforts made by a joint labour–management committee set up in Firestone Textiles of Canada. The committee developed training and retraining programmes to help the employees adjust to a new facility (which was actually a combination and upgradation of two older plants). Similarly, Davis and Lansbury (1987) describe the lobbying efforts of several of the major unions in the Australian communications industry. The unions succeeded in establishing a joint consultative committee, which was to focus on the provision of paid time-off for training, particularly in the adaptation of NIT.

Conclusion

In this chapter, we have examined the various systems of industrial relations practised in different parts of the world, and how these systems have facilitated or obstructed the process of change. Broadly speaking, industrial relations have been classified into two dominant models, namely, adversarial and co-operative. By and large, organizations in the US and in other western countries, with a few notable exceptions, have been found to follow a confrontationist approach in dealing with labour and trade unions, while a more co-operative approach has found favour with those in Japan, Germany and Scandinavia. Industrial relations in India, for various reasons, have been largely based on an adversarial approach, which has constantly suffered from severe conflicts.

We have also discussed how new technologies and their implementation have a direct impact on industrial relations, while industrial relations also influence change in all countries. It must be noted that change in general, and change stimulated by technological inputs in particular, is possible only when there is a minimum degree of cooperation between the different stakeholders, including the management, employees and trade unions. The interface between technological change and industrial relations has been better in those countries where the co-operative model of industrial relations is prevalent. The management and unions in India, where industrial relations have historically been adversarial, could learn important lessons from the successes of certain other countries. The policy statements made by the government, management and trade unions in India in recent years indicate that attempts are being made at a shift towards a more co operative model. Such a scenario may facilitate technological change and structural reorganization. One of the issues that remains uncertain is how far the trade unions will be able to find a new role for themselves in the new scenario.

As we have seen in an earlier chapter, there has been a decline in the membership rates of trade unions worldwide. Several factors, including economic reforms, structural reorganization, technological innovations and ideological issues, influence the unions' ability to recruit members, as well as the workers' inclination to join trade unions. The prevailing legislation, and the attitudes of the government and employers towards the unions are also important. The product and labour markets, technology, and the occupational structure also affect both industrial relations and attitudes and actions of all parties involved. The attitude of the unions, too, determines the capacity of employees to reorganize the workplace as well as their inclination to join unions. Their inclination to join unions may also be affected by the degree of risk involved in doing so, and whether union membership is regarded as the norm or a deviation.

It is generally held that trade unions find it harder to increase their membership during times of economic recession, under competitive conditions (both in the domestic and international markets) and in situations in which there is a surplus of labour and unemployment. In today's situation, trade unions are in an even more difficult position, as firms are bent on reducing production (including labour) costs due to the effects of globalization. At the same time, companies are adopting innovative techniques for the management of human resources, and are working towards the improvement of wages and working conditions without resorting to collective agreements. This, in turn, reduces the role and importance of the unions.

In contrast to the 1980s, the information and communication technology (ICT) of the 1990s has the potential of virtualization.

ICT enables an enterprise to split up its work processes and pool them according to new criteria. It is not geography, but the type of work that becomes central to the functioning of the company. Thus, information related to accounting, for example, can be handled within one geographical space for an entire network of companies. The flows of information which 'create' human work, therefore, constitute new units of collective interests that are different from the classical geographical spaces. In this manner, ICT is often instrumental in enhancing dominance and control through classical Tayloristic separations. However, it can just as well serve as a vehicle for the creation of better jobs for the employees, as well as for an improvement in their skills.

As with any other new development in the area of industrial relations, virtualization has invited debate on whether it (virtualization) represents the end of industrial disputes, or whether it will simply give rise to new forms of conflict which we have not anticipated. It is unlikely that unions will be able to offer collective answers to virtualization on an international basis. This is because they are in a much weaker position the world over, and individualistic ideologies are on the rise. The Scandinavian countries, however, are an exception in this respect. The membership of unions in Denmark has been growing and white-collar workers there are among the best organized in the world. In fact, the recent development of cyber unions being formed by the employees of dot-com companies may mark the beginning of a new era in trade unionism. In the changing economic environment, a spirit of vibrant democracy can be maintained only if the unions formulate active policies on the emerging technologies. Through the active participation and commitment of the employees, trade unions could change the direction of the management of technology.

References

Alberton, M.S, Hancke, B. and Wijgaerts, D. (1990). 'Technology agreements and industrial relations in Belgium'. *New Technology, Work and Employment*, Vol. 5.

Beirne, M. and Ramsay, H. (eds). (1992). *Information Technology and Workplace Democracy*. London: Routledge and Kegan Paul.

Brown, C., Reich, M. and **Stern, D.** (1993). 'Becoming a high-performance work organization: The role of security, employee involvement and training.' *International Journal of Human Resource Management,* 4(2): pp. 247–275.

Case, J. (1993). 'How we will work in the year 2000'. *Fortune,* May 17.

Clausen, C. and **Lorentzen, B.** (1993). Workplace implications of FMS and CIM in Denmark and Sweden. *New Technology, Work and Employment,* Vol 8.

Cooke, P. and **Morgan, K.** (1992). Industry, training and technology transfer: The Baden-Wurttemberg system in perspective. Working paper, Cardiff: Regional Industrial Research.

Cressey, P. (1991). Trends in employee participation and new technology. In R. Russell and V. Rus, *International Handbook of Participation in Organizations: For the Study of Organizational Democracy, Cooperation and Self-Management* (Vol. II: Ownership and Participation). London: Oxford University Press.

Davis, E. M. and **Lansbury, R. D.** (1987). 'Worker participation in decisions on technological change in Australia.' *Labour and Society,* 12(2).

Deutsch, S. (1987). 'Successful worker training programs help ease impact of technology'. *Monthly Labour Review,* November, pp. 14–20.

European Foundation for the Improvement of Living and Working Conditions (1987). *Participation in Technological Change.* Dublin: Shankill Company.

Gann, D. and **Senker,P.** (1993). 'Construction robotics: Technology change and work organization'. *New Technology, Work and Employment,* vol. 8.

Gill, C. and **Krieger, H.** (1992). 'The diffusion of participation in new information technology in Europe: Survey results'. *Economic and Industrial Democracy,* 13 pp. 331–358.

Jain, H. C. (1990). 'Worker participation in Canada: Current developments and challenges'. *Economic and Industrial Democracy,* 11(2).

Japan Institute of Labour (1985). *Technological Innovation and Industrial Relations.* Japanese Industrial Relations Series.

Jones, D. (1992). The productivity effects of employee participation in control and economic returns: A review and some tentative policy implications for emerging market economies. Paper presented at the ILO Conference on Industrial Restructuring, Moscow and St. Petersburg.

Koistinen, P. and **K Lilja, K.** (1988). 'Consensual adaptation to new technology: The Finnish case'. In R. Hyman and W. Streeck (eds), *New Technology and Industrial Relations.* Oxford: Basil Blackwell.

Kuwahara, Y. (1992). 'Technological change and labour relations in Japan'. In M. Ozaki, (ed.), *Technological Change and Labour Relations.* Geneva: ILO.

Lansbury, R. D., Sandkull, B. and **Hammarstrom, O.** (1992). Industrial relations and productivity: Evidence from Sweden and Australia. *Economic and Industrial Democracy,* 13(3).

Levine, D. I. and **Tyson, L. D.** (1990). 'Participation, productivity and the firm's environment'. In Blinder, M. (ed.), *Paying for Productivity: A Look at the Evidence.* Washington D.C.: The Brookings Institute.

Mamkoottam, K. and **Herbolzeimer, E.** (1991): Human resource implications of new technology: A case study of automobiles in Spain. *Indian Journal of Industrial Relations,* 26(3).

Marshall, R. (1992). 'The future role of government in industrial relations'. *Industrial Relations,* 31(1).

McLoughlin, I. and **Clark, J.** (1988). *Technological Change at Work.* Milton Keynes: Open University.

Ozaki, M. (ed.) (1992). *Technological Change and Labor Relations.* Geneva: ILO.

Pot, F. (2000). *Employment Relations and National Culture.* Chelton: Edward Elgar Publishing, Inc.

Rosen, C. (1992). *Employee Ownership and Corporate Performance.* Oakland, California: National Centre for Employee Ownership.

Sabel, C. F. (1993). 'Can the end of the social democratic trade union be the beginning of a new kind of social democratic politics'? In S. R. Sleigh (ed.), *Economic Restructuring and Emerging Patterns of Industrial Relations.* Kalamazoo, Michigan: Upjohn Institute for Employment Research.

Scannell, R. F. (1993). 'Adversary participation in the brave new workplace: Technological change and the Bakery, Confectionery, and Tobacco Workers' Union'. In G. Adler and D. Suarez (eds.), *Union Voices. Labor's Responses to Crisis.* Albany, New York: State University of New York Press.

Simpson, D., Walker, J. and **Love, J.** (1987). *The Challenge of New Technology.* Colorado: Westview Press.

Sorge, A. and **Streeck, W.** (1988). 'Industrial relations and technical change: The case for an extended perspective'. In R. Hyman and W. Streeck (eds.), *New Technology and Industrial Relations.* Oxford: Basil Blackwell.

Tallard, M. (1988). 'Bargaining over new technology: A comparison of France and Germany'. In R. Hyman and W. Streeck (eds.), *New Technology and Industrial Relations.* Oxford: Basil Blackwell.

Tidd, J. (1991). *Flexible Manufacturing Technologies and International Competitiveness.* London: Pinter Publishers.

7
Employee Commitment and Change

As in most parts of the world, trade unions in India too, have not been very enthusiastic to respond to the global challenge. Successive governments introduced major structural reforms on various fronts during the past decades in India. However, the rigid and archaic labour legislative framework has been so far left untouched. Several experiences, particularly those discussed in an earlier chapter, have shown that the attempts to modernize cannot succeed unless it is supported by appropriate human resource policies and industrial relations practices.

As we have seen in the earlier chapters, the Government of India and the corporate sector have taken several steps to cope with the changing realities of globalization and technological change. Our examination of various Indian organizations showed that it is only some companies, particularly those in the private sector, which have succeeded in adopting new strategies to enhance their competitiveness and productivity. It must have become clear from the discussions in the previous chapters that all attempts to change are based on the need and desire to improve performance and productivity. It is equally important to acknowledge the fact that no change is possible unless the employees are convinced of the need for change and are committed to facilitating it. In this concluding chapter, we shall discuss the importance of the involvement and commitment of employees in facilitating any endeavour to change.

The commitment of the employees has always been considered an important condition for creating and maintaining an effective and performance-oriented organization. Today, more than ever, it is widely recognized that an organization cannot grow or perform successfully without the employees' involvement. These days, the survival of organizations (business or otherwise) depends on the

constant updating of knowledge and the renewal of the employees' skills. The 21st century has been characterized as the century of the knowledge economy. Thus, given the growing need
for employees with the requisite knowledge, skills and attitude,
human resources have come to occupy centre stage. This is what
makes it especially crucial for the management to involve the
employees in any proposed changes. In order to do this, all parties concerned must have a proper understanding of what is meant
by employee commitment.

Commitment, in general terms, means being involved. Committed employees display the qualities of dedication, will and enthusiasm when it comes to helping an organization achieve its goals.
Implicit in this is a commitment to all aspects of the organization, i.e., to its products or services, to its customers, shareholders, suppliers, partners and stakeholders, and to fellow employees.
Commitment is considered important for business because it is
expected to enhance employee persistence, by reducing the propensity to leave. It promotes citizenship behavior, in the sense
that committed employees act positively within the boundaries of
their roles and responsibilities. In other words, commitment enhances the organizations performance through the development of
positive attitudes (and interests) among the employees.

Industrial society has witnessed the large-scale growth of organizations, particularly during the 20th century. Max Weber (1947)
advocated the bureaucratic organization as the model organization. He held that this type of organization would be the most
efficient in achieving the collective goals. Modern organizations
came to be symbolized by the engagement and participation of
the workforce, on the one hand, and the management, on the
other. The interaction between these two determines the culture
and efficiency of industrial society to a large extent. The comparatively low level of productivity and efficiency of the Indian
industrial sector is attributed to the absence of commitment
among the workers. In fact, in a worldwide study of employee
commitment, conducted by the Indianapolis Walker Information
and CSM Worldwide Network, Indian workers were ranked ninth,
with a score of 3.77, among the 13 countries surveyed. Canadian
workers got the highest score of 4.19, while Finnish workers got

a score of 4.15. Workers in Spain got a score of 4.14 and those in the US 4.06. An important finding of the study was that the commitment of employees coincided with the extent to which they were attached to the organization. The study discovered that workers in India and other Asian countries (excluding Japan) strongly believed that they would have done better if they had joined another organization (see *Economic Times*, Sept. 20, 1996).

Talking about the criticality of commitment to organizational performance, O'Malley (2000) suggests that commitment, when blended with other ingredients, results in motivation. Motivation may be seen as the result of a combination of factors, including (*a*) a desire to act (commitment), (*b*) an ability to act, and (*c*) an objective. A committed employee will work diligently to improve upon his knowledge and skills, and will constantly endeavour to remove any obstacles that may arise. Commitment is a relationship between the individual employee and the organization in which he works. On the basis of the *Webster Dictionary* definition of commitment as 'the state or an instance of being obligated or emotionally impelled', O'Malley explains that people who are committed feel connected, and are motivated to maintain that connection. He goes on to suggest that a relationship based on mutual commitment would have the properties of psychological attachment. It would be characterized by a long-term altruistic focus, a high level of dependability, and the ability to make constructive and accommodating responses to others. These attributes are, indeed, a great advantage for modern organizations.

Other than pursuing their business goals, modern organizations are also institutions which have a fundamental effect on the employee's way of life, considering that the employee spends a good part of his active life working in the organization. Thus, it affects almost every aspect of an individual's existence. Unfortunately, many modern (work) organizations do not provide an environment in which the individual employee can feel involved or committed. First of all, as observed by Durkheim (1952), the shift from dyadic and face-to-face ties (as seen in a family or in the associations characterizing traditional society), to the impersonal and segmented encounters of industrial life, has weakened the bond between the individual and society. The dissipation of traditional (legitimating) customs and ways of life, and the consequent dis-orientation and sense of being uprooted, is the source of what Durkheim called 'anomie'. Employee commitment can be much better understood if one considers the phenomenon of anomie and alienation. Scholars such as Emile Durkheim, Karl Marx and Etzioni have made immense contributions to our understanding of the modern workplace. We shall briefly discuss some of these concepts and how they can be used to explain the level of employee involvement in organizations, which, in turn, influences the process of change.

Alienation and the Employee's Behaviour

One of the concepts which has a direct bearing on the behaviour of employees is that of 'anomie'. Anomie may be understood to mean the absence of a body of rules which govern social functions. It manifests itself during times of industrial or commercial crisis, and in the conflict between labour and capital. The expansion of the market and the appearance of large-scale industry transform the relations between the employers and workers. Machines replace men, and manufacturing replaces handicraft and small workshops. According to Durkheim, these developments cause a fatigue of the nervous system, which, combined with the contagious influence of large concentrations of employees, increases the employee's emotional and social needs. The employee is regimented, separated from his family throughout the day, and his life is ever more separate from that of his employer. These new conditions of industrial life naturally require the creation of a new kind of organization. However, since the transformation has been so rapid, conflict appears in many forms and equilibrium is difficult to establish.

The concept of anomie can be understood only in the context of the normal conditions from which it is a pathological deviation. The normal would be the normative regulation of industrial relations, and a work situation in which work is meaningful. It is important for a worker to understand the interdependent manner in which he relates with other employees. It is consciousness that makes human beings different from machines; a worker is not a machine, repeating movements without knowing their meaning. He knows that they lead somewhere, i.e., that they lead towards an end which he can perceive of more or less distinctly. Anomie is a deviation from the normal consciousness of the division of labour. Durkheim viewed it as the major cause of all the ills of modern capitalism, and of the routine, degrading and meaningless nature of industrial (and mechanized) work.

Anomie may be seen as the consequence of disaggregation, which weakens the bonds of social relationships and diffuses the collective conscience. The meshes of the social fabric become dangerously slack, alienating the individual from the collective to such an extent that it has no hold over him. Conversely, the individual finds the norms so vague and ambiguous (and perhaps even nonexistent), that there is no moral code for him to draw upon. Anomie springs from the lack of collective force, and the absence of cohesion and a moral order. Anomie is thus a product of modern industrial society, which is characterized by hierarchical structures and centralized systems. Anomie (literally the absence of norms) often results in a situation in which the individual members of an organization feel alienated from each other, besides feeling alienated from the organization. The distance between the employee and his organization has an adverse impact on the organization's ability to achieve its goals.

The word 'alienation', which has its roots in the German language, refers to the state of being estranged or separated from something or someone. Kaufman (1977) describes alienation as a state in which 'something—ties or bonds—connecting man to himself, to others, to the community, and to the technologies and social institutions he has created, is lost, missing or severed, and the state of affairs leads to various pathologies'. The concept of alienation has been used in many ways. It is most often used to convey some form of separation of the individual from some aspect of society, and encompasses a feeling of powerlessness and meaninglessness in professional and interpersonal relationships. Alienation can mean dissatisfaction with one's job (Aiken and Hage, 1966), the experience of unrewarding work (Seeman, 1967), and also, a state in which the individual lacks a sense of self-direction, meaningfulness and self-expression (Blauner, 1964).

Implicit in these diverse nuances is a sense of distrust and distance, which makes the individual feel powerless. The feeling of alienation arises from the absence of commitment and involvement. The employee can feel some degree of involvement if he is allowed to participate in the work process and in decision making related to everyday matters. The employee would definitely feel a stronger sense of integration with the organization if his commitment were sought and valued, though total identification with the organization is not a possibility since it would negate his individual identity altogether. At all events, the prerequisite for understanding why the nature and degree of commitment vary in different organizations/situations is an understanding of the concepts of power and trust.

Components of Commitment

The modern organization and workplace are dominated by decision-making processes and communication systems, in which power plays an important role. In fact, the decision-making process and the system of power, on the one hand, and the communication network, on the other, are interdependent. Decisions are always made on the basis of the information available to the decision-makers. The networks and structures of the organization, both formal and informal, are the channels through which information flows within the organization. Similarly, control is an important aspect of organization life and an essential ingredient to work satisfaction. Closely linked to the concept of power is that of control. When you feel you are in control, you believe that you can influence events and reduce their unpredictability. A sense of control implies the ability to anticipate and regulate conditions that can promote a healthier and more satisfactory work environment. Control, in turn, may be considered to be closely associated with trust. Trust is a psychological state whereby a person is willing to accept a condition of vulnerability on the basis of the expectation that others will behave positively. An important element of trust is predictability, or dependability. Lack of trust leads to a lack of co-operation between different departments and units. This not only results in social disharmony, but also affects the organization's performance. It is difficult to find an organization functioning efficiently if its managers and employees do not trust each other, or if there is no trust among different groups of employees. The case of the Airport Authority of India, discussed in an earlier chapter, illustrates just this.

Trust, or the lack of it, is closely related to the concept of power. It is difficult to foster trust in the absence of an appropriate balance of power between the managers and employees. In fact, the employees' propensity to form and join trade unions may be viewed as an attempt on their part to protect themselves and their interests, particularly when they do not trust their managers. The power structure and decision-making pattern in an organization can also either create or destroy a sense of belonging and commitment among the employees. One of the reasons for the frequent failure of the Indian government's policies to promote efficiency and competitiveness was that the workers did not believe that the policies would serve their interests. On the contrary, they saw those policies as being harmful to their interests. Power may be described as an actor's ability to induce or influence another actor to carry out the former's directives or any other norms he supports. Etzioni (1961) held that an individual's response to power, which he termed '*Compliance*', is a central element of an individual's commitment to an organization. The nature of the relationship between those who have power and the people over whom they exercise power may create either a positive orientation (i.e., commitment) in the subordinated actor, or a negative one (i.e., alienation).

As we discussed earlier, alienation is a state of powerlessness. Such a state arises partly because the power applied on the subordinated actor is not considered legitimate by him and partly because it does not tally with the line of action he considers to be desirable. O'Malley (2000) notes that the employee's commitment to an organization depends on how effectively it fulfils his needs. O'Malley names certain general conditions which could facilitate the development of commitment among the employees. As organizations should also fulfil some important needs of an individual to gain his commitment, they must consider the individual's need for belonging, status (esteem), security (trust), and certain emotional and economic rewards. These general conditions for commitment are briefly discussed below.

- *Compatibility and Belonging.* When the employee's interests and values are congruent with those of the company's, the result is a social milieu in which the employees feel wanted and incorporated by the company. Such a relationship fulfils the employee's basic need for acceptance and inclusion.
- *Status and identity.* When an employee feels that he belongs to an organization and derives value through his association with it, his sense of self (esteem) and status are enhanced.
- *Trust and reciprocity.* The employee must believe that the company is acting on his behalf and that there is a sense of mutual obligation whereby both parties feel an ongoing sense of indebtedness towards each other. Such mutuality creates a sense of security within the employee.
- *Emotional reward.* The employee feels that the organization is conducive to his personal growth, and also finds his work exciting if the work satisfies him and is free of obstacles.
- *Economic interdependence.* When an employee believes that he is engaged in a fair economic exchange, an exchange which benefits him in tangible ways, he derives a sense of sustenance and economic security from the organization.

Thus, O'Malley emphasizes the importance of viewing commitment as a relationship with many components. It may be seen as a composite of feelings which express different levels and kinds of commitment. Such a view (of commitment) also suggests that different forms and levels of commitment can be identified on the basis of the needs of the individual that are being fulfilled in a given context.

The kind of commitment and the type of needs fulfilled by the employees are closely related. Feelings of belonging are associated with a sense of citizenship and affiliative commitment. In this case, the individual feels that his environment is a socially safe one, in which he can voice his suggestions without fearing ridicule. Also, he can acquire new skills without fear of failure. Employees in organizations which encourage a strong sense of belonging are more likely to take on additional roles and responsibilities that go beyond the normal boundaries of their job.

A sense of status and identity encourages persistence and helps to develop association commitment among the employees. An organization's ability to give the employee his rightful status forms one of the binding components of commitment. It impels the employee to stay at work, return to work, and keep on working. As for the components of trust and reciprocity they promote a sense of citizenship and help develop moral commitment among the employees. Employees who are treated well by their employers often want to reciprocate. They will refrain from activities which are injurious to the well-being of the organization. Instead, they will seek ethical and social ends, and try to protect the company from potential dangers and risks. The component of emotional reward is closely linked with performance and helps develop 'affective commitment'. In this case the employees enjoy the activities in which they are engaged. They feel that they are exercising their duties effectively and are satisfied with their vocational/career growth. The better their performance, the greater their enjoyment.

As for economic interdependence, it enhances persistence and helps develop structural commitment. It also helps improve the employees performance. Since the employees are rewarded justly they may refrain from restoring justice by their own methods. Further, employees who are rewarded adequately and are satisfied with their work, are less likely to avoid it by reporting absent or by escaping it through turnover. They may feel compelled to prove their worthiness through creative efforts.

Etzioni's (1961) classification of power and the individuals response to it had certain similarities with O'Malley's classification. He emphasized the fact that an employee's commitment to an organization is affected both by the legitimacy of the employer's directive and by the degree to which the directive frustrates the fulfilment of his needs. He argued that alienation results not only from the illegitimate exercise of power but also from those directives of power which pose obstacles to the fulfilment of the employee's wishes and needs. In other words commitment is generated when the directives are both legitimate and gratifying. Alienation occurs when both these attributes are missing, and the degree of involement is intermediate when only one of the two is present.

Etzioni focused on the involvement of subordinates since the lower a person is in the hierarchy, the more problematic it becomes to gain his commitment. This is because the rewards and perquisites he receives are fewer, and he is in a relatively deprived position. The organization's activities mean less to him as he has little knowledge of what really goes on—from his position, only segments of the organization and its activites are visible. Etzioni saw a direct correlation between the kind of power exercised by an organization and the type of commitment it is able to win from the subordinates. When the power being exercised is coercive, the resulting type of the involvement is 'alienative' (non-commitment). Remunerative power gives rise to 'calculative involvement' (moderate commitment). It is only the use of normative power that can develop 'moral involvement' (total commitment) among the subordinates in an organization.

From a slightly different perspective, commitment has been seen in terms of certain impersonal and abstract principles, including the norms, values and institutions of industrial society. Moore and Feldman (1960) argued that a committed worker is one who has internalized the norms and values of industrial society, and acts accordingly. Education and training socialize the labour force to appreciate the values of industrial society. A committed worker is expected to follow a specific pattern of behaviour in his relations with his co-workers and superiors, as well as his machine.

Machine pacing makes the pattern of work more rigid and curtails the freedom of industrial society. The rigid job boundaries and narrow job descriptions aggravate the employee's boredom at the workplace. The 21st century is already witnessing an increasingly faster rate of technological change. Consequently, skills will become obsolete at a rate faster than ever before, which, in turn, will add to the pressure created by new technology and machine pacing.

Unless appropriate attention is paid to the organizational dimensions, new technologies cannot deliver the full benefits. The complex and increasingly interdependent manufacturing/service systems can function only in a flexible environment. Greater co-operation among employees and ever expanding knowledge, as well as skills for information-processing and decision making will be required to cope with the uncertain environment. The work organization should therefore encourage local autonomy, decentralized decision making and functional flexibility. Functional flexibility and greater degree of functional integration bring together many specalized functional roles. Interdependent systems designed to deal with uncertainties and local diversity would also require greater decentralization of control.

Technological change and the corresponding organizational change would involve a shift in values, norms and the organizational culture. As discussed by Burns and Stalker (1961), it is the *organic* type of organization as against the *mechanistic* organization, which is considered to be most likely to accept technological changes. Organic organizations encourage innovation, lateral rather than vertical communication, higher degree of decentralization, flexibility and integration. Organizational change is found to be easier if all members within the organization share the same values and goals. Such commitment would be characterized by a sense of ownership and participation/involvement of the workers as against the traditional model of organizations where the worker is at the periphery.

Employee Commitment in Mechanistic versus Organic Organizations

The total membership of a concern, which includes its managers, executive officers and workers, constitutes what we call its human resources. These resources and their systematic use determine, to a large extent, how an organization functions. The efficiency of an organization depends on the contribution made by each of its members. Sociologists have mostly used the framework of Weberian bureaucracy to analyze the systematic use of these resources by an organization. A bureaucratic arrangement is characterized by the principles of the division of labour, a unitary chain of command and hierarchy, rigidity of rules, and the separation of personal feelings from official responsibilities. As mentioned earlier, Burns and Stalker (1961) describe such organizations as mechanistic systems.

There are major differences in the type of commitment evoked by mechanistic and organic organizations. In order to gain a proper appreciation of these, let us take a closer look at the two systems. In mechanistic systems, the problems and tasks to be tackled by the enterprise, as a whole, are usually broken down into specialized functions. Each individual is assigned a task, which is then seen to be his duty. Somebody at the top determines the relevance of each member's work to the enterprise as a whole. The technical methods and the power attached to each post are defined precisely, and a high value is placed on such precision and demarcation. There is a clear code of interaction within the organization, which is reflective of a vertical hierarchy between superiors and subordinates. The behaviour of a worker within his prescribed role is governed by instructions and decisions issued by his superiors. This hierarchy of command is maintained on the basis of the assumption that all knowledge regarding the organization, its tasks, and the proper disposition of its human resources rests with the head (Burns, 1969). As discussed earlier, mechanistic systems have proved to be unsuitable in a rapidly changing environment.

Organic systems, on the other hand, are considered to be more adaptable in unstable conditions. When new and unfamiliar courses of action are necessitated, a mechanistic organization will find it difficult to break down and reorganize jobs within its hierachy of specialist roles. In an organic system, however, the methods, responsibilites and powers associated with a job are not so formally defined. No definitive and enduring demarcation of functions is prescribed. All the facts mentioned above have to be constantly redefined through interaction with others. An organic system is a participatory one, in which responsibilities are discharged jointly, and problem-solving is a collective process. Each task, and each individual's role in it, has to be performed with the wider perspective and concerns of the organization in mind. Similarly, the knowledge and skills required for the tasks also have to be kept in mind. The interaction between the organization's members takes place as much laterally as vertically and not within a rigid hierarchy, Thus, communication between people of different ranks can be described as lateral consultation rather than vertical command.

What is relevant here is the kind of commitment that either type of system inspires in an individual. In mechanistic or bureaucratic systems, the worker is clearly told what must be done and how, what he or she does not have to bother with, what is not expected of him and what he should leave to others. Naturally, this lack of participation is not conducive to commitment. In organic systems, on the other hand, the individual is allowed to feel fully involved in the discharge of any responsibility; he is valued not merely in terms of his competence, but also in terms of his commitment to the success of the concern's undertakings.

Tom Burns argued that the variety of commitments into which an individual enters, is bonded by his identity as a person as well as his career. The variety of institutions and representations in the workplace re-duplicates those affecting the working environment. The type of commitment, further, reflects the value system of the individual as well as of the culture to which he belongs. When an individual acts (in a job situation), he selects or determines the sort of performance he will put in and the role he will act out, or he decides to merely carry out the imperatives of the job. The individuals ability to determine the social significance of his behaviour in this way presupposes the existence of a plurality of action systems, according to Burns (1969). The fact that he makes these choices presupposes that he can order these action systems preferentially. However, such preferential decisions are also influenced by the managerial practices within an organization.

As we saw in the cases of the NAA and DOP, a mechanistic work culture does not inspire commitment among the employees and ultimately proves to serve as a hindrance to the process of change. However, once the DOP's top management made concerted efforts in various directions, including the management of its human resources, it was able to initiate substantive changes, though in a gradual manner. Other companies, like HLL, Britannia Industries and Eicher Tractors Ltd, won the allegiance of their employees only after they introduced certain changes in their mode of functioning—notably, productivity bargaining. The same can be said of SAIL, which introduced important changes to gain the commitment of its workers. In sum, organizational rigidity (mechanistic systems) does not make for employees commitment.

Human Resource Management and Change

It is obvious by now that unless an organization manages its human resources properly, it cannot hope to gain the commitment of its employees. It has taken years to appreciate the full import of this. The approach to the study of employees' behaviour at work changed radically with the rise of the human relations movement in the late 1940s, following the path-breaking Hawthorne experiments (Mayo, 1945) and the emergence of organizational behaviour as a distinct area of knowledge in the late 1950s. Gradually, the field's intellectual centre of gravity came to be firmly grounded in the discipline of organizational/social psychology. The attention of the scholars shifted from a macro-level discussion of the productivity of employees to the micro-level problems concerning an organization's culture and the participation of its employees. Employees began to be viewed as the organization's assets or human resources, which soon led to the emergence of the field of human resource management. The rapidity of technological change, the growing importance of IT and the increase in global competition during the 1980s and 1990s gave rise to new strategies of managing human resources. The management in India, too, started focusing on sharing information, improving communications, involving the employees in problem-solving, improving the quality of work life, and reaching out to workers to build a relationship of trust with them. This is amply illustrated in Ramaswamy's (1994) study of Rayon Spinners.

Arbitrary practices regarding recruitment, deployment, promotion and reward systems have proved incapable of creating motivation among the employees in India, as elsewhere. Often the supervisory and managerial personnel do not possess the requisite knowledge, skills or orientation to deal with their subordinates. Indian organizations are lacking as far as scientific planning of manpower and sound policies on industrial relations are concerned. Many managers perceive of trade unions as hostile institutions and attempt to circumvent, if not totally avoid them. The short-term gains of the management are often given precedence over long-term strategies for developing a competent and committed workforce. This is extremely detrimental to the process of change, as the best agent of change is a committed worker. Therefore, as reflected in the recent management theories and research, human resources, have to be constantly nourished and carefully maintained.

According to Cappelli (1999), there has been a decline in the importance of commitment to the company in terms of loyalty. At the same time, research findings suggest that if an organization encourages employee participation, it enhances the employee's sense of commitment (Mathieu and Zajac, 1990). Further, when employees are convinced that their employer is concerned about their well-being, they display a higher level of commitment (Eisenberger et al, 1990). In fact, the meaning of the term commitment itself has undergone a change. A recent study by Singh and Vinnicombe (2000) of senior engineers in three major engineering companies in the UK and Sweden indicates that today, commitment means having a highly proactive and innovative approach to work, as part of a mutually beneficial psychological contract with the organization. It also implies the willingness to take up challenges at work. In other words, commitment consists of the employee's capability and readiness to face the challenges of change. Only a positive work culture can foster this sort of commitment.

The best way to promote such a culture is by encouraging a healthy, productive relationship between the organization and individual employees. Such a relationship may be built up by nurturing those aspects which are conducive to commitment, by reinforcing the set of conditions which yield the outcomes desired by the organization. Here, it would be appropriate to mention the conditions named by O'Malley, which are belonging, status and identity, trust and reciprocity, emotional reward, and economic we reviewed earlier. Commitment serves as an appropriate and convenient organizing construct and besides all the other advantages mentioned earlier, it helps to build the readiness to cope with change.

This brings us back to the importance of appropriate strategies of human resource management in this age of rapid change. If an organization inspires its employees' commitment by carefully nurturing and developing them as key resources, it will be much better equipped to introduce qualitative changes in its culture and work practices. As mentioned earlier, the management of personnel and industrial relations should not be regarded merely as a fire-fighting system, but should be restructured and viewed as integral parts of a holistic strategy of human resource management. This strategy has to be evolved at the highest level of the management. The thrust of the new human resources policy should be to attract, retain and develop human resources on a continuous basis, so as to attain corporate excellence and maintain the organization's competitiveness.

We have already mentioned several ways in which an organization can involve its employees in its functioning, and thereby, gain their commitment. In short, we had mentioned the need to foster a new work culture, encourage teamwork and decentralize decision making. In addition, the management should make specials efforts to understand the worker and his union. It is equally important, therefore, that the managers should develop social skills to communicate more effectively with the subordinate employees and their unions. A positive and professional approach is required for the management of the employees' grievances and the negotiation of collective settlements. Through a combination of all these measures, the organization can improve its chances of coping successfully with its increasingly unpredictable environment. To cite the example of a large engineering concern, the management recently engaged in long-drawn negotiations with the union. Ultimately, the working hours were reduced, from 47 to 45 hours per week and the wages were increased—steps which resulted in a 10 percent increase in productivity.

Ray Marshall (1992) had suggested that systems which perform will involve their employees, to a significant degree, in what have traditionally been considered 'management' functions. An organization can enhance its productivity, improve the quality of its services/goods and achieve flexibility, provided that the employees are fully involved in the process. The same results can be obtained if decisions regarding production are made as close to the point of production as possible. It must also be remembered that in order to effect change, the unions and management must stop seeing each other as rivals. Even in West Bengal, a state where labour has traditionally been militant, the left-controlled CITU welcomed 'participatory management'. The general secretary of the state unit of the CITU said, 'If the workers are involved in the technological upgradation process, their resistance to modernization will stop'. The emerging pattern of human resource management and industrial relations in India reflects a growing realization by the management, employees and trade unions that they can survive in a competitive environment only if they learn to cope with a constantly changing environment. Organizations will be able to cope with the challenges of change if their human resources are committed to the process and implications of the change.

References

Aiken, M. and **Hage, J.** (1966). 'Organizational alienation'. *American Sociological Review*, 31(4).

Blauner, R. (1964). *Alienation and Freedom*. Chicago: Chicago University Press.

Burns, T. (Ed). (1969). *Industrial Man*. Harmondsworth: Penguin Books.

Cappelli, P. (1999). *The New Deal at Work*. Boston: Harvard Business School Press.

Eisenbeger, R. Fasto, P. and **David LaMastro, V.** (1990). 'Perceived organizational support and employee diligence, commitment and innovation'. Journal of Applied Psychology 75(1): pp. 51–59.

Durkheim, E.(1952). *Suicide*. London: Routledge and Kegan Paul.

Etzioni, A. (1961). *Modern Organizations*. New Delhi: Prentice Hall.

Josephson, E. and **Josephson, M.** (1974). 'Alienation: Contemporary sociological approaches'. In F. Johnson (Ed.), *Alienation*. New York: Free Press.

Kaufman W. (1977). Introduction In R. Schacht (ed.), *Alienation*, London George Allen and Unwin.

Marshall, R. (1992). 'The future role of government in industrial relations'. In M.F. Bolgnanno and M.M. Kleaner (eds), *Labour Market Institutions and the Future Role of Unions*. Massachusetts: Blackwell.

Mayo, E. (1945). *The Social Problems of an Industrial Civilization*. Cambridge, Massachusetts: Harvard University Press.

Moore, W.E. and **Feldman A.S.** (eds). 1960. *Labour Commitment and Social Change in Developing Areas*. New York: Social Science Research Council.

O'Malley, M.N. (2000). *Creating Commitment*. New York: John Wiley and Sons.

Ramaswamy, E.A. (1994). *The Rayon Spinners*. Delhi: Oxford University Press.

Seeman, M. (1967). On the personal consequences of alienation in work. *American Sociological Review*, 32(2).

Singh, V. and **Vinnicombe, S.** (2000). 'What does commitment really mean? Views of UK and Swedish engineering managers'. *Personnel Review,* 29(2): pp. 228–254.

Weber, M. (1947). *The Theory of Social and Economic Organization.* Glencoe, Ilinois: Free Press.

Index

About the author

Kuriakose Mamkoottam is Professor of Human Resource Management and Industrial Relations at the Faculty of Management Studies, University of Delhi. He has a Master's degree in Sociology from the Delhi School of Economics and a Ph.D. from the University of Delhi for his work on personnel management and industrial relations. He earlier taught at the Delhi School of Economics and the Sriram Centre for Industrial Relations and was India—EEC Fellow at ESADE, Barcelona. Apart from his teaching, he has been a consultant and trainer with a large number of organizations including the International Labour Organization, the Bangladesh Employers' Association, Nestle, The Indian Oil Corporation, Department of Posts, BHEL, Eicher, TELCO and Hero Honda. He has published numerous research papers and is also the author of two books: *Trade Unionism: Myth and Reality* (1982) and *Managerial Trade Unionism* (1990). His research interests include worker trade unionism, managerial unionism, ethnoagriculture and new technology and human resource management in India, South Asia and Europe.